Working with Statistics

Working with Statistics

An Introduction to Quantitative Methods for Social Scientists

Stuart Reid

Polity Press

First published 1987 by Polity Press
in association with Basil Blackwell.

Editorial Office:
Polity Press, Dales Brewery, Gwydir Street,
Cambridge CB1 2LJ, UK

Basil Blackwell Ltd
108 Cowley Road, Oxford OX4 1JF, UK

British Library Cataloguing in Publication Data
Reid, Stuart
   Working with statistics: an introduction to quantitative methods for social
      scientists.
   1. Social sciences — Statistical methods
   I. Title
      300'.28   HA29

      ISBN 0–7456–0047–6
      ISBN 0–7456–0048–4 Pbk

Typeset in 10 on 12pt. Palatino
by Columns of Reading
Printed in Great Britain by
Page Bros. (Norwich) Ltd

Contents

List of Tables

List of Figures

Preface

I once began a handout for students taking an undergraduate Statistics course with the statement that 'Statistics is a compulsory course for First Year . . .'. In typing this I managed to omit the 'o' from 'course', leaving a statement which, however unintentionally, expressed, I suspect, far more accurately the sentiments of the students themselves. The evident unpopularity of statistics as a subject for those primarily studying one of the social sciences is due in part to the (normally unjustified) fear of anything mathematical among students who have opted for 'Humanities', and in part to the isolation of statistics from the rest of the subjects studied in such courses. Regardless of how easy the writers of textbooks can make statistical procedures appear, the relevance of these to the rest of the student's education often remains mysterious and unexplained. Students who enjoy studying the theories of the state, the sociology of medicine, or industrial relations, may find it hard to understand why they should know how to draw a bar chart or calculate a standard deviation. The objective of, and justification for, this book is to present basic statistical techniques of value to the social scientist *within the context of their use*. In doing this I shall also present an argument for statistics as both an integral part of sociological knowledge and a rewarding element in its practice.

Statistical procedures are used in undertaking, and analysing the products of, research. The analysis is important, since many social scientists (not to mention the interested general public) who undertake little or no research of their own still rely on the research of others in order to acquire new information, to assess arguments and to generate fresh theories of social life. The ability to understand how a particular set of figures was arrived at, and to criticize the way in which it was produced, helps considerably in producing an accurate and useful evaluation of research and the claims deriving from it. Moreover, we are living in a world in which the development of comparatively inexpensive and easily used computer equipment has extended both the degree and the nature of data analysis. On the one hand statistical information, especially in computerized form, is being more widely used; on the other hand, computer technology has made such information more accessible to the individual researcher. Accordingly, I have included in this book not only a discussion of the organization of data for computer analysis but also a guide to some of the computer programs available to the social scientist.

The book also diverges from the normal practice in statistics textbooks by utilizing a single set of data for examples. This has two advantages: firstly, the student encounters statistical techniques in the course of an evaluation of a real research project; secondly, the value of these techniques should become more obvious when applied to a set of data with which the reader can become progressively more familiar. The normal practice of proliferating different examples, from different kinds of research, has always seemed to me to be both confusing and unrepresentative of the use of statistics in real-life research.

Ultimately, then, this is a book which, while wishing to teach basic technical skills, equally is intended to communicate the fundamental usefulness of statistics to the modern social scientist. I hope that it enables the reader to acquire some of these skills not just painlessly but with a positive enjoyment of the practice of statistical research and analysis.

Acknowledgements

I would like to thank Claire Bakes at Brunel University for advising on the text and for overseeing the SPSS procedures, Tony Giddens for initially suggesting the book (and then turning a blind eye while its production lagged), and Elizabeth Garnsey at Cambridge University for giving the early chapters a sympathetic reading. I would also like to thank Rosemary Crompton and Gareth Jones of the University of East Anglia for granting me permission to employ data produced during my work with them in 1979–80.

Last but not least I wish to thank the many students who attended the S110 course at Brunel between 1980 and 1986 and who enabled me to learn with them. This book, its merits and its faults, is dedicated to them.

S.R.

A Note to Readers

If you wish to use this book as an introductory text in the teaching of statistics to social scientists, or as an aid to self-tuition, then it is particularly highly recommended that you do so within a framework that includes the use of microcomputers. Indeed, much of the data analysis can be reproduced using computer programs and packages and the reward in terms of active involvement, not to mention the valuable skills acquired, is substantial.

Appendix 1 contains the database used in the majority of examples and can be utilized in following the material in the book. Alternatively, other databases could be used in a similar way, permitting students to work through a series of procedures using a single set of data. Many of the examples provided here in the figures and tables were produced using SPSS (Statistical Package for the Social Sciences) on a mainframe (large, centralized) computer, but others were performed on an Apple IIe microcomputer, and all of the operations covered in this book can be performed using relatively simple computers with the appropriate programs. More details of suitable programs and computers are given in appendix 4.

Readers may also be interested in the source of the data used in the examples in this book. They are authentic, and only very slightly simplified, data produced originally in the course of a research project sponsored by the ESRC. The particular material used here derives from one case study of a large administrative bureaucracy and consists primarily of 'background' information – grade, sex, age, length of employment. This sort of information was produced for all employees before more complex attitudinal and work-task studies were carried out. Although the study made extensive use of questionnaire interviews, most of the background data was gathered directly from the organizations' own records.

Further exercises using the book

To gain the greatest advantage from the book, it is suggested that a course of practical exercises is pursued, utilizing the database and following through both the examples provided in the text and the additional exercises offered at the end of each relevant chapter. The first step is to enter the database and/or the sample database (see Appendix 1) on to a computer; this is dealt with at the end of chapter 3. Thereafter the material can be studied, to some extent, at the user's own pace. The Further Exercises are comparatively simple suggestions to provide more familiarity and therefore confidence with each new set of procedures.

1 An Argument for Statistics

1.1 Introduction

It has not always been fashionable in recent years to espouse the cause of statistical sociology. The great founders of this tradition have been rigorously and repeatedly criticized for the conceptual and technical shortcomings of their statistical approach to the study of social phenomena. *Quantitative* sociology (the use of measurement in the analysis of social behaviour and attitudes) has been too closely associated with 'positivism', the school of thought founded in the nineteenth century which is now regarded as crude and misguided in its attempt to create a 'science of society' analogous to the sciences of the physical world. Criticism of positivism has gone hand in hand with a growing enthusiasm among sociologists for the more *qualitative* aspects of social investigation – small, detailed studies, participant observation, in-depth interviewing, textual and linguistic analysis – sometimes referred to as *interpretative* or *hermeneutic* sociology. As a consequence, quantitative work has attracted little status and too few social scientists have acquired the statistical and analytical skills that go with this branch of the discipline.

In order to avoid the isolation of quantitative analysis from sociological theory it is necessary to teach statistical skills as an integral part of the study of sociology and as a vital prerequisite for those undertaking social research. The ability to plan productive research, to organize and analyse data meaningfully, and to present both quantitative and qualitative information in a way which is both honest and free of jargon, is invaluable. This is more true than ever today, when, on the one hand, so much statistical information is collected and yet, on the other, so little effort is made to expose such statistics to rigorous examination. In the sections which follow I shall look briefly at the use of statistics in the history of sociology as a discipline, and then at the way in which statistical analysis provides a valuable instrument for the commentator on social life.

1.2 Historical background

The development of sociology and the evolution of statistical techniques to measure and analyse social life had a common origin in the social welfare studies of Victorian philanthropists. Many now familiar techniques such as questionnaire interviews had been pioneered by the state through agencies such as the Registrar General (collecting data on death and illness), the Factory Inspectorate and, of course, the decennial Census of Population first taken in 1801. But it was wealthy individuals who carried out the seminal studies in which the collection and organization of statistical information were explicitly used to test hypotheses about the social conditions of the time.

Much of the impetus for statistical sociology in the Victorian Age came from people's desire to understand, and thus to control, the social world which was changing so rapidly around them. Central to this attempt to comprehend the transformation of society was the application of scientific method: scientific knowledge, and its application in technology, was a primary motive force in the industrialization process and it appeared logical to the Victorians to employ similar methods in the analysis and management of human behaviour. Moreover, the claim to be 'scientific' lent a status and legitimacy to sociological study which its relative novelty and enterprise might not otherwise have commanded.

Most of the earliest social analysts not only constructed grand theories of societal development within which their contemporary changes could be explained, but did so in a manner or with a method which they claimed was 'systematic' or 'scientific'. The Frenchman Auguste Comte (1798–1857), normally credited with the invention of the word '*sociology*', declared that in politics, imagination should be made subordinate to 'observation'; Karl Marx (1818–83) characterized his study of historical development as the scientific study of 'the laws' of society, in much the same way as Newton had established the 'law' of gravity, or Victorian scientists were concerned with the laws of chemical, physical or astronomical activity. Marx's friend and collaborator, Friedrich Engels, undertook one of the first great studies of the urban poor in Victorian Britain,[1] and Marx drew heavily on the statistics produced by the state, particularly those of the Factory Inspectors, in his examination of the relations between employer and worker in the new industrial world.[2] The idea was enthusiastically propounded that there could be a science of society directly analogous to the sciences of physical or chemical matter. English writers such as Herbert Spencer (1820–1903) followed Comte in linking this idea to a view of history and knowledge as progressive, linear processes in which a science of society would be at once both the means of understanding and of improving the social world.

Statistical information came to be regarded as the raw material of this new science and the accumulation of 'facts' about the conditions of social life became a preoccupation for the Victorian pioneers of statistical study. Such a preoccupation, sometimes to the exclusion of more careful theoretical thinking, was to generate a backlash against the faith in a science of society and its methods of statistical quantification. As sociology became, in the twentieth century, both more sophisticated and more self-critical, so its methods became more varied and its pretensions somewhat more modest. I shall discuss this at greater length below; suffice to say here that the backlash may at times have gone too far in deriding the nevertheless valuable work of the Victorian champions of statistical investigation.

By the end of the 1840s both Britain and America had Statistical Societies and the use of the social survey (in which professional, trained interviewers are used to elicit information from selected respondents) had become a recognized tool of the new science. The British government had created the post of Registrar General to oversee the production of social statistics and such information had been explicitly related to issues of law and policy-making.

This work had, however, already gone beyond the accumulation of numerical data for the purpose of description alone. Medical researchers such as W. Farr and E. Chadwick had collected statistics on death and illness rates which were differentiated by the sex, age and social position of the respondents. In this they were anticipating one of the major uses of sociological investigation: the attempt to explain variation in the behaviour, attitude and environment of individuals and social groups. Much of what has followed, particularly in the field of statistical analysis has been directed towards the refinement of our ability to measure such variation.

One more vital step had to be taken and this was achieved in the work of the Victorian social investigators, epitomized by Charles Booth. It was Booth who set out not just to investigate the conditions of the urban poor through the employment of statistical study but, crucially, to use the information which he would produce to assess an explicit assumption, or hypothesis, about contemporary life. The 'Hungry Forties' had greatly accelerated the concern of both the government and individual philanthropists with the conditions of the urban poor in the great industrial cities and had aided the development of basic sociological tools – the questionnaire, the research interview, the statistical table, the comparison of differing social groups – but it had not eradicated many of the prejudices held by the Victorian upper and middle classes about the nature of poverty. Specifically, Booth set out to question the assumption that poverty was the result of the individual's own lack of effort, in the great age of self-help and individual achievement, it was generally accepted that the indigent was a figure to be scolded or instructed, not understood or sympathized with.

Booth, however, largely rejected the fashionable notion that poverty was the result of idleness and, instead, concluded that for the great majority of those living in poverty their condition was determined by factors such as ill health, unemployment or large family size, which were mostly beyond their power to prevent or correct. Not only is the conclusion a characteristically sociological one, stressing the *social* rather than *individual* determination of poverty, but the methods employed to reach that conclusion were precursors of much of what we would now recognize as the tradition of survey-based statistical research.

> . . . for the first time in sociology a researcher had tested a hypothesis about social life by collecting facts . . . Throughout the nineteenth century the commonly accepted belief was that poverty was caused by idleness . . . The explanations were individual not social . . . Booth showed, for the first time, in a way that made it difficult to gainsay him, that the cause of poverty was social not individual. It was questions of circumstance or questions of employment not questions of habit. The social world was opened to study.[3]

It would not be exaggerating to say that a great proportion of the statistical skills you will learn and use as a sociologist will serve the same purpose as those used by Booth: to better describe and understand the social world; to test outdated, contentious, compla-cent or palpably erroneous assumptions; to clarify the determinants of social conditions, behaviour and opinion. Neither the basic methods nor, indeed, the moral purposes have been rendered obsolete by time or criticism. On the contrary, the refutation of a commonly held misconception, especially one mobilized for political purposes, through the careful and imaginative analysis of social phenomena, has remained one of the most valuable (and consequently one of the most maligned) attributes of sociology. It is one to which statistical skills can make a rich contribution.

It would be unfair to give the impression that Booth was alone in this pioneering work. Many others shared Booth's concerns and his enthusiasm for investigative methods: famous figures such as Henry Mayhew (1812–87), whose *London Labour and the London Poor* (1851 and 1861) anticipated many of the techniques and concerns of Booth, or Seebohm Rowntree, whose *Poverty, a Study of Town Life* was published three years before Booth's major work. Even more famous, but not normally in a sociological context, is Florence Nightingale, who was a passionate accumulator of numerical data in her unprecedented work as a nursing administrator. One of her biographers[4] described her as 'a master of statistics' and certainly she was able to quantify the effect of her efforts in the Boer War by monitoring the death rate in the army hospital under her command.

Many accounts of the use of statistics in sociological research begin with the French sociologist Emile Durkheim (1858–1917), whose work on suicide rates has been generally considered to be the single most important book in the canon of quantitative research. Without detracting from Durkheim's work, it is salutary to recognize the work of these early survey researchers in England, particularly given the fact that Durkheim's work was not translated into English – and thus not widely accessible – until 1933. Although Durkheim, unlike Booth and his contemporaries, was self-consciously a sociologist (and, indeed, did much to shape sociology as an academic discipline) and made far greater use of explanatory concepts and theoretical speculation, the Victorian philanthropists had anticipated much of the core of his work in their ability to place numerical data in a theoretical context, using it to clarify and explain as well as to describe. Indeed, we find Mayhew in the 1850s[5] constructing statistical tables to assess the correlation between illiteracy and delinquency as part of a debate upon the 'moral improvement' provided by schooling for the poor.[6]

R.A. Kent, in his history of British empirical sociology,[7] raises the question of why this early research did not produce a cohesive school of English sociology much earlier than the eventual founding of the Sociological Society in 1903. His answer lies in the priorities of most of these Victorian researchers, which were social accounting and reforming rather than the development of social theory and explanation: there was little or nothing to tie the many strands of endeavour together.

> Innovations tended to be isolated events, unrecognized and unperceived as such by contemporaries and successors alike. Many were forgotten, perhaps only to be 'discovered' decades later as if nothing like them had been known before. The social accounts never were committed to the development of a science of society; their objective was social reform.[8]

It was the work of three mathematicians, F. Galton, K. Pearson and G.V. Yule, in the last two decades of the nineteenth century, which provided the basis for most of the techniques of correlation which are still in use today. When the Victorian social investigators had assessed the influence of one factor upon another (e.g. unemployment on level of poverty) they had to rely on close scrutiny of their tables of cross-classified elements. The techniques of correlation, regression and measures of association developed by these mathematicians permitted an estimation of probability in the relationship between social attributes which went significantly beyond the researcher's simple observation.

In 1912 another mathematician, Arthur Bowley, produced a paper which heralded another giant step forward for statistical sociology: he described the use of statistically based sampling techniques in a social survey. Hitherto, although many of the Victorian investigators had, in effect, taken samples of particular populations, the grounds for doing so had lacked any mathematical evaluation. Bowley pioneered the procedure for selecting samples on a mathematical (and thus more reliable) basis and, as Professor of Statistics at the London School of Economics from 1919 to his retirement in 1936, became one of the greatest influences in the teaching of statistical techniques.[9] By the time of the First World War, therefore, the greatest part of what we now recognize as statistical or quantitative sociology had been established.

This, however, was to be something of a false start, and many of the trails opened by both those such as Booth and Bowley were to be left unexplored until after the Second World War. Instead the impetus for the advancement of social statistics shifted to the United States where quantitative analysis found, and has continued to find, more consistent favour than in Europe. Whereas Britain could still, in 1951, only boast one Professor of Sociology, in America there were said to be 50 such academic positions by the year 1908.[10] Moreover, the teaching of empirical research methods became an integral part of many American university courses both at under-graduate and postgraduate level. It was also in America that many of the innovations and refinements in techniques were now to be developed, including perhaps the most significant of all – the utilization of electronic data processing in the analysis of social information.

From the massive mainframe computers of the immediate post-war era to the incredibly cheap and sophisticated mini-computers of the present day, the electronics industry has made complex statistical analysis an everyday reality for the social scientist. Many of the widely used procedures of modern research analysis rely upon the ability of the computer not only to handle large amounts of data at great speed, but to perform complex calculations with a precision and reliability beyond all but the most dedicated human statistician.

As in the dawn of statistical sociology, it has been the agencies of the state which have often made the most extensive use of such facilities and, indeed, have precipitated their rapid evolution. The monitoring of social life through the collection and production of social statistics has become a minor government industry yet, as we shall see later, the form, content and presentation of these 'official statistics' leaves much to be desired by the conscientious social researcher. The use of computers by sociologists themselves, normally through the medium of specially prepared 'packages' of statistical programs, is also beset with problems, not least the danger of substituting impressive data manipulation for inadequate data. In fact, we find ourselves now in a world where the possibilities for statistics are enormous yet the knowledge and skill necessary to exploit that potential are still not widely held or exercised.

Whereas in other branches of social science, notably economics, psychology and some branches of management studies, sophisti-cated statistical techniques have enjoyed a central place in the discipline's development, many areas of sociology have been much slower in utilizing the advances made in statistical analysis. The advent of computer-based packages which contain a large range of statistical techniques suitable for sociological data has also in some instances created a division of labour between the sociologist and the computer programmer or adviser, in which the former is perhaps excessively dependent on the latter for the execution of procedures which the researcher understands only partially. Now the availability of microcomputers with increasingly imaginative programs, and the shift to 'decentralized' computing (in which the researcher/user can be in control of every stage of data entry and analysis), presents an opportunity for social scientists to utilize the undoubted power of contemporary techniques without the intrusion of an 'alien' world of computer specialists.

Beyond factors such as the sheer speed of data processing, the major advantages provided by modern statistical techniques and computerized processing have been in the management of complex numerical information. Whereas the pioneering social researchers relied on relatively simple statistics such as percentages to evaluate the effect of one factor upon another, it is possible now to measure a large number of elements simultaneously in order to assess which factors in a situation are trivial and which important. There have also been advances in the social scientist's ability to judge the reliability of data, to test how representative the data are, how significant a particular finding might be. But all of these techniques rely for a proper understanding on an initial grasp of why, when and how quantitative analysis is used: technical and electronic wizardry can never be a substitute for sociological understanding. As Kent has remarked,[11] 'the very power of statistical programs available on contemporary computers can tempt researchers to produce factors of no theoretical relevance, or to make nonsensical statistical "explanations".'

1.3 Statistics, sociology and 'science'

I have already mentioned a number of times that the kind of quantitative survey research espoused by both the Victorian philanthropists and the 'positivist' sociologists has come in for fairly thorough and often acerbic criticism. The origin of this criticism lies in the rejection of Comte's notion that sociology could become a science of society comparable to the physical and natural sciences. Critics of this assumption have emphasized the crucial differences between the social and the natural world and the consequent inappropriateness of the scientific methods of investigation and conclusion proposed by the positivists. The object of sociological study is, after all, not an inanimate thing but a complex network of human beings who are conscious of their situation and thus are able consciously to change it.

This has other, even more profound, implications. The work of the sociologist takes place in a social world which is constantly being created or re-created by human actors – of which, of course, the sociologist is one. The phenomena which sociologists study may *seem* to be external to them, as suicide rates did to Durkheim, or urban poverty to Booth, yet they are never more than *products* of the actions of human participants in a huge, complex web of affairs which includes the sociologist as well. Consequently, when we study social life we can only understand it as a fellow participant, not as a wholly detached scientific observer: In this sense a science of society can never imitate the model of the physical sciences which so impressed the Victorians.

The nature of sociology's subject-matter has also rendered the pursuit of 'laws' governing social life a fruitless quest. Although it would be rash to claim that social behaviour is not in many instances both structured and predictable, we cannot expect human action to be repeated with the exactitude and certainty which is seen to mark elements of the natural world.

> Besides the seeming certainties, the system of precise laws attained in classical mechanics, that model for all aspiring sciences . . . which in the nineteenth century was unquestioningly assumed to be the goal to be emulated, the achievements of the social sciences do not look impressive.[12]

This further implies that the hopes of those such as Marx or Comte who saw a science of society as not just clarifying the structure but facilitating the transformation of the social world must equally be disappointed. Indeed, as we shall see, our claims for even the most rigorously handled research analysis must always be cautious. Sociologists have learned to talk in terms of probabilities rather than certainties, of what is rather than what should be.

It is interesting, and pertinent here, to note that the natural sciences themselves have also come under fierce scrutiny during this century. Indeed, part of the criticism of the social sciences derives from the work of writers whose main concern has been to show that the nineteenth-century model of scientific endeavour is an inadequate account of how all or any scientists really work.[13] In short, then, we can no longer pursue a quantitative research programme with the self-confidence and certainty with which the early statisticians treated their methods and their findings. Our instruments of investigation, of measurement and of analysis are, to be sure, far more sophisticated and powerful now, yet we must use them with a delicacy which acknowledges the unique situation of the researcher into social life.

1.4 The value of statistics in contemporary sociology

Where, then, does this place statistical sociology in the contemporary world, and why, more immediately, should we learn how to manipulate numbers in the understanding of something – society – which can never be measured by numbers alone? The first mistake to avoid in this discussion is the confusion of quantitative or statistical research with positivistic sociology. To wish to measure aspects of social life numerically no longer implies a belief in the 'scientific' nature of one's work, or in some determinist view of history. Instead, it implies a belief in the usefulness of statistical methods when attempting to order and comprehend the complexities of substantial bodies of data. It is first one of the tools which social scientists have at their disposal: appropriate to some bodies of information more than others, and to some forms of analysis more than others, but nonetheless valuable in conjunction with the other tools of the social scientist's trade, from theoretical speculation to linguistic analysis.

Ultimately all sociology derives from some form of observation of society and its constituent members. The sociologist, as we have already noted, is part of society and thus even the most speculative idea, made prior to any actual research project, will necessarily rely upon concepts, impressions, statements or observation already gleaned from that same society. When we undertake social research we simply make a more systematic attempt to understand a particular area of social life, an attempt in which our role as observer becomes more self-conscious and more ordered, and in which our role as participant/member becomes more controlled yet, possibly, more difficult. In this process of systematizing our observation of social life, statistical techniques can aid the researcher in three important respects. These are:

(1) measurement
(2) comparison, and
(3) the control of uncertainty

The first two functions have been central to social investigation since nineteenth century; the third, however, has been the era in which twentieth-century statistical knowledge has made its most significant contribution. Let us look at these one by one.

(1) *Measurement*. Our first impressions of any data are gained from fairly simple counting. This may be the calculation of how many respondents in a questionnaire survey were male and how many female – a relatively unproblematic matter – or how many firms in a study of, say, computer companies employed more than 250 workers. The latter should also be a simple calculation but, unlike the former, cannot so easily be checked by a researcher carrying out the study. Many of the early social surveys, and much of the information produced by government departments, are primarily concerned with such calculations: the recording of the number of privately-owned houses in the country, or the calculation of the proportion of the population drawing the old age pension, or the number of people killed each year in coal-mining accidents. Such information is represented in the sort of descriptive statistics with which most of us are familiar – percentages, proportions and averages.

The act of measurement is, however, rarely this straightforward. Most of the things which we want to measure in social research require careful definition *before* we can record and quantify them. Even the apparently simple examples above are evidence of this: before we could calculate the number of privately-owned houses we would have to decide on our definition of 'privately owned' (e.g. would it include private houses rented out to other people?) and of 'house' (would it mean any household, or would it exclude flats, holidays homes, houses used for businesses . . .?). Such decisions of *definition* may still not present major problems, yet when a sociologist tackles an issue such as social class, satisfaction at work or mental illness the importance of a satisfactory definition becomes paramount. Indeed, one of the recurrent objections to the quantifying of such concepts is precisely that social actors hold very different definitions of these things and that we cannot be confident that what we are measuring is indeed a consistent or clearly identifiable phenomenon. This is not, however, a justification for abandoning measurement so much as for refining our definitions and clarifying the relation between our general or theoretical concepts, the definitions we develop, and the manner in which these are used in research. Chapter 2 deals with these issues in greater detail, in the context of the planning of a research project.

I have been referring so far to data gathered in an original piece of research, but frequently a sociologist will want, or have, to utilize data produced by an agency over which little control can be exercised – a government department, another sociologist, an independent research unit. Here, measurement is also beset with the problem of *recording*. That is, we want, as far as possible, to know when, where and how information was recorded. Unfortunately, much statistical information is not produced with the sociological researcher in mind and the theories and definitions behind the initial recording of data may be obscure to the person studying the data at one remove. There is, however, a more positive side to this view of official statistics. Some government data is now being made available in its 'raw' state, with explanations of research methods and definitional decisions. The link between academic activity and official research shows signs of growing stronger, with consequent improvements in the usefulness of the data.

Before we can measure, then, we need to define, or at least to ascertain to the best of our ability someone else's definitions, and to make clear the link between what is intended as the object of study, the definitions employed, and their relation to our theories and conclusions.

(2) *Comparison.* The sociologist always wishes to go beyond mere description, and the first step beyond is *comparison*, both within a particular study and, subsequently, with information from other sources. The most obvious way in which statistics can aid comparison is by allowing the researcher to select groups of particular interest and compare their characteristics. Take the example of coal-mining injuries. Having first established the nature and reliability of our statistics and considered broad descriptive data (e.g. annual number of mortalities, injuries attributed to certain causes), we would want to compare factors which might be influential. Variations between each year, between different periods of the year, between regions, between different types of work – all of these and many more would have to be carefully extracted and assessed. Some data may need to be standardized (i.e. turned into a standard form in which it can be compared with other data) in the form of percentages, rates (e.g. number of injuries per 1,000 employees in a region) or indices. As a result of such manipulations the researcher will both see a clearer picture of the data, and begin to isolate those factors which are important, and to investigate these further. Later in this book I shall show how researchers use statistical techniques both of great simplicity and of great sophistication to undertake this sociological detective work.

(3) *The control of uncertainty*. In the seminal studies of mass society, the researchers had few ways of checking on the reliability of their information. They could be, and sometimes were, painstaking in their selection of appropriate sources from which to gather data, and meticulous in their performance of interviewing, processing and analysing these data. Nevertheless, they could not measure their data in order to say, for example, whether variation between responses was significant in some way or due merely to chance. Nor could they assert with any confidence (though some still did) that the individuals, groups or areas of their studies were good bases for generalization about larger sections of the population. Much of the statistical advance in this century has been in the development of techniques to measure and control uncertainty. Statistical procedures can help us to evaluate whether variations in our data should be regarded as important or as relatively trivial; whether our group of interviewees are typical of a larger group from which they were drawn and, if so, how typical. What statistics cannot do, and we should be forever mindful of this, is to *prove* anything. The notion of a final, incontrovertible proof is as alien to contemporary sociology – or indeed, to the broader discipline of statistics – as it was congenial to nineteenth-century positivists. In the modern world scientists of all kinds must deal with matters of probability, not proof, and are more aware of the dangers involved in making universal claims for the findings of limited investigations. Social statistics can help the social scientist to assess probability, and to say with what confidence that probability can be stated. This may not be the science of society for which our predecessors wished but, in the analysis of social life, it is scarcely an implement which we can discard or ignore.

Summary

The use of statistical techniques in the study of social life is not, in its present form, a very old practice. Its origin in state censuses, social investigations and the studies of the positivist sociologists bequeathed a legacy which quantitative sociology has often found a burden. Statistics alone could never make sociology a science and the techniques of numerical measurement have always encountered problems in the study of social rather than physical life. Partly as a consequence of its inability to meet what were, with hindsight, impossible expectations, statistical work – in Europe in particular – now enjoys a rather less exalted status. Combined with the anxiety which its mathematical components engender in prospective social scientists, such disfavour has too often isolated statistics from other branches of social study. Isolation as a form of study has led to isolation in practice, with statistical skills being too often left to specialists, particularly with the added need for computing skills to utilize the statistical programs available to the sociologist. Such a trend needs to be reversed.

Statistics has some simple advantages to offer the student of social life and provides a mode of analysis which is invaluable in the management of large bodies of data and yet sensitive enough to be applied to a great range of different sorts of information. We are as apt to require statistical sophistication if we are employed to study the implications of social research as if we are employed to undertake that research. The reader of the newspaper needs to understand graphs, tables and averages just as the specialist social scientist does. The political commentator needs to know how to turn government statistics to advantage by criticizing not just a politician's conclusions but the 'facts' upon which they are based. In many such respects the origin of statistics in the work of Victorian philanthropists should not be entirely scorned: we still wish to understand and control our social world; and statistics, though it can never take decisions for us, might at least help us to judge what decisions are to be made. Chapter 2 explores further the place of statistics in the process of social investigation and, in particular, emphasizes the necessity of locating statistical analysis within a methodological framework which recognizes both the origins and limitations of quantitative data.

Notes

1 F. Engels, *The Condition of the Working Class in England* (St Albans, Panther Books, 1969; first published in England, 1892).
2 For example, see K. Marx, *Capital*, vol. I (Harmondsworth, Penguin Books, 1976; first published, 1867) p. 411 sqq.
3 G. Easthope, *A History of Social Research Methods* (London, Longman, 1974), p. 55.
4 E. Longford, *Eminent Victorian Women* (London, Weidenfeld and Nicolson, 1981), p. 88.
5 For an interesting account of Mayhew's status as a pioneering sociologist, see Eileen Yeo's essay 'Mayhew as a social investigator', in

E.P. Thompson and E. Yeo, *The Unknown Mayhew* (London, Merlin Press, 1971). Yeo points to Mayhew's extensive use of statistical information and his employment of interviewers and statistical assistants in his surveys of the London poor.

6 See ibid., pp. 32–3.
7 R.A. Kent, *A History of British Empirical Sociology* (Aldershot, Gower, 1981).
8 Ibid., p. 29.
9 It is interesting to note that while Bowley, much of whose work focussed on sociological phenomena, occupied the LSE Chair of Statistics, the Chair of Sociology was shared between Westermarck and Hobhouse, both primarily philosophers! For a fuller account see Kent, *British Empirical Sociology*.
10 Ibid., p. 121.
11 Ibid., p. 201.
12 A. Giddens, *New Rules of Sociological Method* (London, Hutchinson, 1976), p. 13.
13 See, for example, T. Kuhn, *The Structure of Scientific Revolutions* (Chicago, University of Chicago Press, 1970). For a discussion, see Giddens, *New Rules of Sociological Method*, chapter 4.

2 Methodological Considerations

2.1 Statistics as a social product

There is some confusion nowadays in the usage of the words *method* and *methodology*. Let us distinguish them here. *Method* refers to the technical procedure by which we undertake an investigation, from the general style of research (e.g. postal questionnaires, analysis of government data, in-depth interviewing) to the final details of statistical analysis. *Methodology* is the body of knowledge and ideas which provide our understanding of how, why and when we use sociological methods. Much of this book is about method; much of this chapter is about methodology. In practice the two are inseparable. It is no more possible to have statistical method without methodological understanding than it is to have the materials for building a house without the architect's conception of what the house will be. In considering methodological issues we prepare ourselves for the effective and constructive use of method.

Statistical data are neither produced nor utilized in a social vacuum, free of the interests, values, prejudices and pressures of human actors. Indeed, in any one research project the final shape of the data may be influenced by the interests of the researchers themselves but also by the organization funding the research, by any additional staff employed in the research, such as interviewers, coders, statistical or computer consultants, and of course by any individuals or groups who find themselves the subject-matter of the research. Each of these parties will contribute to the appearance of the data in its final form, yet the person encountering the completed project's 'findings' may be tempted to treat them as figures in some pure form, 'gathered' by the researchers and utilized in the scientific evaluation of a particular theory or hypothesis. The researchers themselves may, knowingly or otherwise, connive in such an interpretation – these are, after all, *their* data and, as such, precious to them. Such impressions need to be dispelled. Research is a process, not just a technical process but a social process in which social forces mould the outcome. Statistics are best seen, then, as the product of this process, created by the decisions and actions of all those involved.

Even the normal vocabulary of empirical research tends to mask the reality of data production: we talk of statistics being 'gathered' or 'collected' as if they were firewood waiting to be picked up and carried home. Similarly, statistical techniques are commonly treated as neutral instruments of data collection and analysis, free from the taint of values or bias. Yet, every technique we use has advantages and limitations which affect the nature of our data, just as every aspect of method is the result of a policy decision taken by those controlling a project.

> . . . statistical practices are social in nature and their conceptual and technical instruments, orientation and uses all need to be seen in social terms . . . statistics are not collected, but produced; research results are not findings, but creations.[1]

However, as the authors of the above statement point out, this is less an argument for avoiding or abandoning statistical research than for improving our methods of understanding and undertaking such work.

> The complex statistical end-product is therefore no arbitrary creation; it is rather more in need of being explained than either being taken for granted or dismissed.[2]

Once we have understood that statistics are products of our decisions and actions as researchers, then we can improve both our own research planning and our analysis of others' statistics. Any set of data becomes more than a presentation of information in numerical form and can be regarded instead as the embodiment both of the information itself and of the theorizing, value-judgements and categorizations of those who produce it. As Hindess has said, 'The evaluation of social statistics is never reducible to a purely technical evaluation.'[3]

2.2 Statistics in the research process

Some of the methodological issues that arise prior to the technical procedures of quantitative research and analysis must now be considered. There are four 'levels' at which the researcher must take decisions about any study: the ethical, the theoretical, the conceptual and the operational. In effect, these amount to a progressive narrowing of the researcher's focus from very broad moral considerations towards the specific technical decisions of the research performance.

2.2.1 Ethical decisions

Part of the criticism of the positivist tradition of social science has been directed at the assumption made by early social investigators that their methods were scientific and therefore neutral and unbiased. The claim to value-neutrality or moral objectivity has only been reluctantly abandoned and the pioneer sociologists, including Max Weber, certainly believed that it was possible, within carefully observed rules, to prevent the values and prejudices of the researcher from colouring the conduct and findings of the study. Similarly, there was little concern in the early days of the discipline about the ethical implications of studying society: researchers were not particularly troubled by the effect their research might have on those being studied.

In the twentieth century all this has changed. Firstly, the critique of positivism has made it abundantly clear that social scientists cannot dissociate their own values from their research activity; indeed, in a very real way, the value-judgments – explicit or otherwise – made by the social scientist are an integral and important part of the research process. Secondly, this increased self-awareness has prompted a greater awareness of the ethical questions raised by the relationship between researcher and subject, interviewer and respondent, the student and the studied. In short, no research programme can begin or continue without some serious consideration of the value of the researchers themselves and the consequences of the research for those otherwise involved.

Of course, it is not only the values of the social scientist that are important: the other parties to the research (sponsors, respondents, research employees) will also hold values which may influence the research process and cannot be ignored. As Barnes has written,

. . . each of the parties in the process of inquiry is certain to have its own interests and values, its own expectations or lack of them, about what may or should emerge from the inquiry, and maybe its own ideas about what is morally right or wrong in making inquiries into social phenomena.[4]

These values are not only relevant at an abstract, moral level of decision-making but can also constitute practical constraints which will determine what the researcher may be willing, or may be permitted by others, to do.

Such considerations were not a major problem for Victorian social scientists, fortified both by their adoption of a natural science model of research (neutral scientists studying passive phenomena objectively) and by their position of social superiority over the people they were studying. The essential inequality of the research relationship was instrumental in reinforcing the positivist view: the labouring poor were hardly likely to question the moral right of a Victorian gentleman scientist to inquire into their degradation, and he thought it as much his right to do so as the early anthropologists felt confident in their right to intrude into the lives of hitherto unstudied tribes and civilizations. The notion of a relationship between scientist and subject that was two-way, interactive and equal had not been considered and it is one which is still sometimes forgotten!

Thankfully, it is no longer acceptable to treat individuals or social groups as akin to inanimate objects freely available for the scientist to observe. The relationship between the student and the studied is now less frequently characterized by an inequality of power and social status[5] and, perhaps crucially, the power of those who sponsor social research and those (Barnes calls them 'gatekeepers') who permit social scientists access to organizations or groups they wish to study, has increased substantially. That is not to say that such ethical questions have been unequivocally resolved, but that the superordinate position once bestowed upon the scientist by knowledge and status can no longer be taken for granted by any of the parties involved. Social scientists today are dependent on the money, cooperation and goodwill of a number of other parties whose view of life in general, and of social inquiry in particular, may not coincide with their own. This necessitates not just a serious consideration of one's own values as a researcher, but a consideration of the influence those values may have on the research and on the participants in that research and, furthermore, of the influence which the values of others may have on one's own research practice.

One particular source of the reassessment of ethical decisions has been the political uses to which social science, and the evidence of social scientists, has been put. It is not difficult to realize, with a twentieth-century world-view, that the incursion of an anthropological research team into a remote area may have many serious social consequences for the area's inhabitants, far beyond the novelty or inconvenience of the study itself. Similarly, the sociologist interviewing office workers in a modern corporation will be aware that those employees have a view about sociology, may even have studied it themselves, and may be deeply suspicious of any connection the sociologist appears to have with their management or employer.[6] However, the ethical and political implications may not be so obvious either to the participants or, sometimes, to the scientist.

Social scientists organizing their own research with funding from a source which might at least be assumed to be independent, such as their own university or an autonomous funding agency, may be well able to evaluate the moral, political and ethical issues raised by their work. However, the production of statistical information has commonly been financed by less disinterested bodies. This has become increasingly true in the twentieth century as sociologists and others have been employed by governments, companies and other institutions rather than working as independent individuals. As Pahl notes, in his article 'The sociologist as a hired expert',[7] the employment relationship places the sociologist in a difficult role in which his information or advice may be judged not on its quality but on its acceptability or usefulness. At an extreme, such a role can raise very serious ethical questions for the researcher, as happened in the now notorious Project Camelot, in which social scientists were employed by the United States Department of the Army to study the sources and resolution of conflict in Latin American countries.

> It was seen as a basic research project, aimed at identifying the preconditions of internal conflict and at discovering the effects of action taken by local governments in easing, exacerbating or resolving these preconditions. . . . The project was based on the assumption that increased knowledge . . . would enable the United States Army to cope more effectively with internal revolutions in other countries.[8]

From Barnes's description the issues raised by the research seem fairly clear, and fairly disturbing. Yet the project was cancelled primarily due to external pressure from Latin American governments, not because of the concern of the scientific community.

If the initial motivation for employing social researchers can be open to ethical and political question, then the use of statistics generated by research requires even greater moral caution. One of the most common, though often ill-judged, criticism of statistics is that they can be, and are, used to prove anything their authors care to prove. Certainly the potential for misuse of statistical information is enormous and Huff amusingly catalogues some of the ingenious forms of misrepresentation in his excellent book.[9] But there is nothing intrinsically deceptive about numbers: indeed their inter-pretation should be easier than the interpretation of words, loaded as the latter are with ambiguities of meaning. But most people are a good deal more literate than they are numerate and, moreover, have been brought up to think that numbers have a single meaning. Consequently, statistics are treated as either self-evidently true or self-evidently false: statisticians are either credible scientists or manipulative charlatans. To get at the usefulness which lies between these extremes, numerical information requires not just a wider education into the use and abuse of statistics, but the development of a critical view which sees statistics as the outcome of a process in which motives, meanings and methods become embodied in the final data, and thus must be included in any analysis. Confronted with any statistical material we need to ask:

(i) Who produced it, and when?
(ii) Why was it produced?
(iii) How was it produced?
(iv) What is actually being presented here?
(v) What does this material mean?

If the context of the statistics cannot provide answers to those questions we have every right to be suspicious of their meaning. A good example is provided by Brown in his account of research into the effect of violent video films on young children.[10] Engaged by a rather amorphous group of churchmen and members of the House of Lords to conduct a survey of children's exposure to video films, Brown found himself and his research team under pressure to produce results that could be used to influence an ongoing parliamentary debate on obscene and violent videos. More disturb-ingly, he claims that research published under his name bore little or no relation to material that his unit had produced and that the final report relied heavily on statistics, the origins of which were not explained. Brown regarded the whole exercise as an example of apparently respectable, scientific social research being used to give credibility to a wholly political argument which could not be, and had not been, verified by full and careful investigation.

The production of statistics does not take place in a moral vacuum but in a social world where the values of the social scientist have consequences for the character and meaning of the statistical data; the nature of the research, both in its performance and its publication or utilization, has consequences for all those connected with it, or effected by it. In turn, the behaviour of the social researcher is influenced by the other parties to the research, particularly the funding or controlling agency: such influence stretches beyond the instigation of the research to its performance and to the presentation of any findings.

2.2.2 Theoretical decisions

> . . . the world is a vast sea of potential data in which one could swim aimlessly in perpetuity (or drown) without criteria for selecting and organizing the data. These criteria are provided by the problems and theories derived from sociology.
>
> (M. Bulmer, *Sociological Research Methods.*
> *An Introduction* (London, Macmillan, 1977, p. 3)

In chapter 1 it was argued that the value to the social scientist of a quantitative approach to the analysis of the social world lay in the potential which statistics provide for the ordering, measuring and clarifying of information in the assessment of theories, assumptions or claims which might otherwise be contestable only at the most abstract level of philosophy. Clearly, if this is to be the purpose of statistical sociology then its practice must go considerably beyond the mere description of data, however useful that may be as a starting-point. The social researcher is trying not just to describe but to understand and explain social phenomena and, to do that, needs to interpret the world through a frame of reference of some kind. In other words, the proper practice of research can only take place within the guiding framework of theory.

The development of one's theoretical frame of reference should be fairly well advanced before beginning any empirical research in exploration of those theories. Poorly thought-out theory can lead to poorly planned research: it is important that the choice of research techniques, the definition of concepts and the form in which the data will be produced are all appropriate to the theoretical intent of the research. There is no automatically correct form of research procedure and no single model of research that is universally applicable: it is the theoretical concerns of the social scientist and the problems with which the study is concerned which primarily influence the selection of concepts, techniques and presentation. Statistical research is a process of decision-making and many of these decisions will be guided by the theories with which the research begins.

> One commonly hears statements to the effect that it is the purpose of research to test hypotheses developed theoretically and that statistical methods enable us to make such tests. It must be realized, however, that the processes involved in getting from theory to actual research hypotheses and from these hypotheses to probability statements of the kind used in statistical inference are by no means direct. In both cases certain decisions have to be made, decisions which may lead to considerable controversy.[11]

Indeed, it would be misleading to suggest that most, let alone all, researchers begin with a clear-cut theoretical hypothesis. For many researchers theories may start life as just the most general, and vaguest, speculations about the connection between particular social phenomena. Alternatively, one may begin with a sense of unease about theories or explanations put forward by other sociologists, or perhaps, simply, with a desire to investigate an area of social life which appears to have been unduly neglected, or repeatedly misjudged. Even at the most exploratory, descriptive level, however, the scientist needs theories to place boundaries on the investigations and to provide a sense of direction. This requires the formulation of some broad theoretical statements. Take the example of Charles Booth mentioned in chapter 1. Booth's desire to undertake social research was prompted initially by his observation of, and concern for, the extent and degree of urban poverty in Victorian England. At this stage the interest was no more than that: Booth began to read, observe and collect information about poverty. This lead him to consider specifically theoretical explanations of poverty, particularly the widespread notion that the poor are themselves primarily to blame for their condition. This notion could then constitute a hypothesis which could be tested empirically.

The movement from a general theoretical enquiry to identifiable hypotheses (in which a relationship between two or more factors is presented as an explanation of social conditions or behaviour) is necessarily a process of selection and decision-making. For any broad area of interest (poverty, class, industrial action, leisure, race, education) there are an infinite number of theoretical statements which might provide the stimulus for empirical research. Each general theoretical statement might in turn give rise to a number of more detailed hypotheses to be investigated. In taking selective decisions of this kind the sociologist is not just guided by personal interests, or the interests of the funding agency, but by considerations of time, resources and methods. The first two constraints are fairly self-explanatory: a study of poverty might ideally cover the whole nation, but in practical terms might have to be concentrated on a particular area accessible to the researcher which would provide an appropriate source of material. The relation between theory and method is perhaps less well documented.

Bulmer criticizes the teaching of research methods for assuming that these methods are 'a set of skills which can be learnt and applied regardless of context'.[12] On the contrary, he argues, method needs to be closely tied to theory and the technical procedures of research selected in the light of the theoretical problems they are intended to illuminate. At the stage of the formulation of theory and research hypotheses it is necessary to raise the question of technical strategies. We need to ask what sort of data would be appropriate for evaluating our theoretical statements. How should such data be collected? How much detail do we require? In what form should the final data be produced? Which factors are going to be most crucial? What background information should we collect to provide depth, and allow for other possible influential factors? Such questions will enable the researcher to make choices between, say, a large-scale survey of a wide area, or an intensive study of a limited area; between including or excluding certain groups from the study; between ignoring or recording pieces of related information; between recording data in broad categories or in precise numerical detail.

Left to a later stage of the research, the relation between theory and method can result in the production of statistics which cannot 'fit' the problems which the researcher is addressing: the data may have been organized in a form which makes it possible to test certain key hypotheses; certain factors may have been only cursorily recorded, yet prove, on analysis, to be potentially vital to explanation. No researcher can allow for all of the modifications necessary in an ordinary research project, nor for the play of the unexpected which upsets prior plans and assumptions. But a consideration of methods at the stage of theorizing can at least optimize the match between the two.

2.2.3 Conceptual decisions

It should be clear from what I have already said that the process of research is by no means a cut-and-dried scientific progression, but rather a sort of dialogue between researcher and research, in the presence of practical and intellectual constraints, which progresses by a series of problems, decisions and compromises. Arguably the most difficult stage of that dialogue is the creation of concepts and categories by which we order the social world which we observe.

Much of the critique of quantitative sociology has centred on the problem of conceptualizing social reality, and of subsequently defining that reality in terms of sociological categories.[13] All theoretical statements contain concepts which serve to represent aspects of the social world. In the example of Booth's research, the most important concept is 'poverty': it may seem at first encounter an unambiguous word used to describe a particular state of human affairs, a condition of social life. However, in common with all concepts, poverty is an historically and culturally variable term with no precise or universally accepted meaning. What constitutes poverty in one society may constitute wealth in another; what constitutes wealth in one century may constitute poverty in another. More crucially, any one society or any one age may measure a unique set of factors in order to assess poverty; to describe someone as poor can only make sense if the listener shares with the speaker a complex set of cultural assumptions which allow both to understand the same thing by the word 'poor'.

Although theory may begin by utilizing a concept, the definition of which is nebulous or assumed, it cannot progress very far until some conceptual clarification has taken place. This is vital both because theories cannot be tested or evaluated by others if the constitutent concepts remain woolly; and because the data which we produce will be organized and structured according to the concepts and categories selected as the focus of the research. As I have already emphasized, statistical data are not value-free 'facts' waiting to be 'collected': the form of our data depends on our own research decisions. It is not hard to imagine two concepts of poverty, for example, which produce quite different sorts of data. One re-searcher may conceptualize poverty as an exclusively economic condition, defined in terms of a certain level of net income and access to related material resources: the data produced will be in the form of statistical measures of income. A second researcher may conceptualize poverty as a condition of social life arising from material deprivation but crucially involving elements of social deprivation (e.g. lack of personal mobility) and of psychological deprivation (e.g. feelings of frustration and hopelessness): the data produced will include scales measuring mobility or frustration, and categories recording the feelings and perceptions of people in the study.

The way in which we define a concept therefore determines the nature of the information produced to represent that concept. Confronted with a limitless social world to investigate, the sociologist unavoidably makes decisions which order fragments of that social world into categories, and henceforth refers to those ordered fragments as concepts. Very few conceptual definitions can be taken for granted; most must be defined in the course of an investigation. Certainly some concepts will have a sufficiently clear and commonly-agreed meaning that they will require little or no elaboration. Most members of any society will understand the same thing by the concept 'age' for example, or 'birthplace', but even these assumptions cannot be made if the social scientist is operating in an unfamiliar culture.

Very commonly also in social research we are dealing with the responses of individuals interviewed in the course of research. This introduces another element of uncertainty into our categorization of data: how does one know that the respondent (interviewee) understands the same thing by a particular concept as the researcher (interviewer)? As Cicourel has said, sociologists often rely upon 'common-sense concepts that reflect common knowledge known to both sociologists and the "average" members of the community or society'.[14] The danger inherent in doing this is that the meanings of concepts become assumed rather than defined in the context of a theoretical framework. In other words, instead of carefully defining what 'poverty' means and then recording information to measure it, the researcher gathers information on the assumption that 'poverty' means the same to both researcher and respondents. Clearly, this is an assumption which often cannot be safely made. Mayntz, Holm and Hoebner emphasize that shared meanings can never be taken for granted: 'In each case one should first consider whether the concepts central to a research project are so unanimously used that an explicit definition is unnecessary.'[15] Working with most sociological concepts necessitates the thorough definition of meaning before embarking on the production of statistical data.

2.2.4 *Operational decisions*

I have already suggested that the end product of any research project will be powerfully influenced by the normative, theoretical, and conceptual decisions made in the planning of the research: the more careful and thorough this planning, the more valuable and useful the final data are likely to be. In particular I have tried to stress how the recognition of one's own values and interests is a necessary part of preparing a quantitative study. The positivistic model of sociology, with its emphasis on scientific objectivity and the neutrality of the researcher, has given way to a model of sociology which recognizes that sociology itself is a social process which, like everything else in our social world, is guided by people's interests, beliefs and values. To accept such a view of sociology is not, as some have assumed, to abandon the attempt to measure social life statistically: rather, it requires a form of quantitative sociology which is more self-aware, more explicit in its operation and more rigorous in its definitions.

The last of my four areas of decision-making concerns the most detailed stage of this process of definition. Having defined the relevant concepts in the context of a theoretical framework, these concepts must be expressed in a form which can be utilized in the practice of research itself – in interviewing or observing social phenomena. The concepts must have an *operational* definition.

> It is not enough, in empirical research, for the relevant central concepts to be explicitly defined. Precise directions for research procedure must be given by means of which it can be determined whether a reality exists corresponding to a given concept.[16]

These precise directions are the operational definition, and constitute the detailed categories in which data will actually be organized. Accordingly, these categories must be explicit and unambiguous in their definition; they must, as far as is possible, be comprehensible to any participants in the research, and must be replicable by other researchers if necessary.

> Operational definitions . . . are definitions that actually spell out the procedures used in measurement. . . . Since all measurement involves classification as a minimal requirement, an operational definition can

be considered to be a detailed set of instructions enabling one to classify individuals unambiguously.[17]

With a basically quantitative concept, such as age, our main concern will be to produce categories which are unambiguous and which record all the available information in as useable and accurate form as possible. For example, we shall have to decide whether to measure individuals' ages in years or in years and months, or simply to record their actual date of birth. Categories may be single ages (25 years old, 26 years old, etc.), or broader groupings (over 25, over 30, etc.) in which case the boundaries of each category must be exactly defined (e.g. does the category 'over 30' include 30-year-olds or not?). Such detailed decisions are necessary to ensure consistency and reliability of recording. Additional problems are raised by more qualitative concepts, that is, ones which do not obviously lend themselves to numerical measurement. Here, the researcher must often analyse what constituent parts make up the concept and decide whether these parts can be separately measured.

For instance, a purely economic definition would consist of a series of categories representing different levels of gross or net income. But a more wide-ranging definition of poverty may include qualitative concepts such as hopelessness. To measure this sort of concept requires an examination of how such feelings might be expressed in social behaviour: we might decide, for example, to measure how often respondents go out of the house, or visit friends; how often they apply for a job and how they rate their chances of getting it. In other words we construct a number of practical *indicators* which are measurable, and use these indicators to represent our concept. Obviously, such a process is highly selective and risks omitting important information, yet it does enable the researcher cautiously to measure concepts which otherwise might remain undefined or, worse, used as if their meaning was commonly shared and unproblematic.

One very general word of warning needs to be sounded about this whole process of decision-making and definition. The undertaking of a research project will, unavoidably, bring to light inadequacies and inaccuracies in the theoretical, conceptual and operational decisions made by the researcher. Some data simply will not 'fit' categories which were designed to record the anticipated information; some phenomena will emerge as far more important than expected; concepts which seemed crucial to the researcher may appear meaningless to the other participants in the project. This is why social scientists normally carry out *pilot studies* in advance of the main study in order to assess the accuracy and usefulness of the definitions they have constructed. But even after the modifications engendered by the pilot study the research procedures cannot be assumed to be in their final form. There should always be *feedback* between the process of research and the instruments used in the research. It may be that slightly different methods would yield more useful information; the pilot study may not have shown up weaknesses in certain definitions; the situation in which the study is being carried out may have altered. This does not mean that the form of questions or the definition of concepts should be repeatedly changed: indeed, that would dangerously undermine the consistency of the study. But the researcher must be prepared to interpret the data produced as a result of the interaction between research procedure and research subject: any major failures should be recognized rather than perpetuated. As Hindess has written, without categories it is impossible to define and order the world we observe; yet no categories can exist entirely independent of what they have been formed to record.

> If we were to send into the field a team of ideal observers, stripped of all concepts they would return with nothing to report and no vocabulary with which to report it. Any proposed set of categories can only be evaluated in terms of existing knowledge.[18]

Summary

The practice of statistical research and analysis is not the collection and subjection of ready-made facts to neutral, scientific techniques of analysis. It is a social process in which the decisions, interests and values of all concerned in that process contribute to the appearance of the statistical data in their final form. Decisions have to be made at a series of levels – moral, theoretical, conceptual and operational – which determine the procedures to be used and the form in which information will be produced. At any time during the production of data feedback may compel reassessment or modification of these decisions. Figure 2.1 represents this process in a simplified form.

The consequences of this process of decision-making may seem even more obvious if we consider the problems involved in analysing statistics produced by other people. Presented with a statistical table showing, for example, the number of people living in

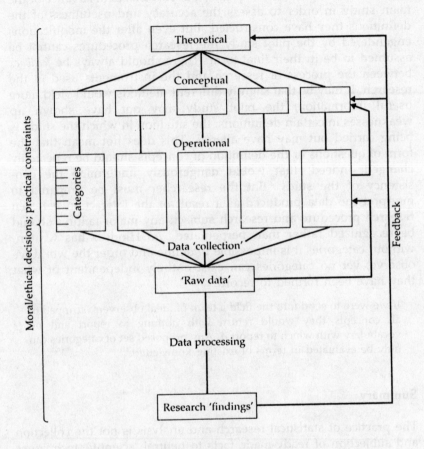

Figure 2.1 *A diagrammatic representation of the research process*

The whole research process is circumscribed by evaluative considerations and practical constraints which shape the purpose and scope of the research, the ethics of its execution, and the control of its final presentation. Within this the broad theoretical interests give rise to the identification of key concepts. These in turn must be defined and translated into operational definitions. The categories of these definitions shape the data produced in empirical research and data analysis. Each stage of the process produces potential feedback for evaluating earlier stages. This diagram, necessarily, gives a neat and schematic representation of what, in practice, can often prove an untidy and complex process!

poverty in Great Britain for each of the last ten years, it would be necessary to reconstruct the decisions made in the production of the table. First, one would ask who had produced the statistics, when and for what purpose: the possibility of particular values or interests influencing the information would have to be assessed. Second, one might want to know whether these data were produced as part of a wider investigation and, if so, what were the guiding motives behind that investigation. What hypotheses, for example, were being explored? More specifically, how were the concepts used in the research defined – what was meant by poverty in this context? Ideally, one would look for the operational definition of the concepts, and the original categories in which the data were organized. Finally, one would have to examine how the data were presented – was the table an accurate representation of the data? In other words, the process shown in figure 1 has to be followed analytically when assessing the 'findings' of others' research. Statistics are always the product of such processes and must always be evaluated with this in mind. We can never divorce sociological (or any) data from the process of its production.

> Measurement is a theoretical problem; for the purpose of measurement is that of classifying and ordering reality. How one orders reality is a theoretical question. The simplest measurement problem is to decide whether or not a piece of observed reality does or does not interest the sociologist. What is, or is not, of interest . . . is of course a key theoretical question. . . . If a sociologist seeks to construct a scale in which some aspects of reality score higher than others . . . then he is in fact suggesting a theory of social reality which sees reality as an hierarchical order. *Underlying all measurement systems therefore are theoretical assumptions about the nature of social reality.*[19]

With such considerations firmly in mind we can now move on to learn some of the basics of statistical methods and their employment in sociological analysis. The first step in doing that is to become familiar with the new vocabulary and new concepts essential to the discipline of statistics.

Notes

1 J. Irvine, I. Miles and J. Evans, *Demystifying Social Statistics* (London, Pluto Press, 1979).
2 Ibid., p.3.
3 B. Hindess, *The Use of Official Statistics in Sociology* (London, Macmillan, 1973), p. 47.

4 J.A. Barnes, *Who Should Know What?* (Harmondsworth, Penguin Books, 1979), p. 15.
5 Although the tradition of British sociology, certainly, has continued to be primarily interested in the situation of economically, socially or politically disadvantaged groups.
6 It may be salutary to consider an example from the author's own experience. While conducting an entirely independent survey, I was refused access to certain employees by their managers who, acting as gatekeepers, had decided that my presence might disrupt staff-management relations. They insisted that I should only contact individuals outside working hours and to this end provided a list of their employees' home addresses. They did this, however, without consulting either the employees or their union: the consequence was that many employees refused to co-operate with the survey and, within the company, the union initiated a grievance procedure against management for their disclosure of individuals' addresses. A simple lack of ethical consideration served to defeat the purposes of both gatekeepers and sociologist.
7 R.E. Pahl, 'Playing the rationality game; the sociologist as a hired London expert', in C. Bell and H. Newby (eds), *Doing Sociological Research* (London, Allen and Unwin, 1977).
8 Barnes, *Who Should Know What?*, p. 47.
9 D. Huff, *How to Lie with Statistics* (Harmondsworth, Penguin Books, 1973).
10 B. Brown, 'Exactly what we wanted', in M. Barker, *The Video Nasties* (London, Pluto Press, 1984), and idem, 'Nasty report that left out the factual niceties', *The Guardian*, 24 September 1984.
11 H.M. Blalock, *Social Statistics* (2nd edn, New York, McGraw-Hill, 1972), p. 11.
12 M. Bulmer, *Sociological Research Methods: An Introduction* (London, Macmillan, 1977).
13 Most famously, A. Cicourel, *Method and Measurement* (New York, The Free Press, 1964). For a critical evaluation of this school of thought see Hindess, *Official Statistics*, chapter 2.
14 Cicourel, *Method and Measurement*, p. 20.
15 R. Mayntz, K. Holm and P. Hoebner, *Introduction to Empirical Sociology* (Harmondsworth, Penguin, 1976), p. 16.
16 Ibid., p. 17.
17 Blalock, *Social Statistics*, p. 12.
18 Hindess, *Official Statistics*, p. 40.
19 G. Easthope, *A History of Social Research Methods* (London, Longman, 1974), p. 121. Emphasis added.

3 The Vocabulary
of Social Research

Before one can learn a language a certain amount of basic vocabulary has to be acquired: even simple communication requires the combination of a limited structure and content. Statistical skills are a language of understanding and of communication through which we translate data into as concise and comprehensible form as possible so as both to understand their meaning and to communicate our interpretation of that meaning to others. This chapter sets out to provide some of the basic terms and categories of meaning which are essential in carrying out statistical analysis. Much of what is covered relates directly to the discussions in the two preceding chapters and will also prepare the ground for the statistical work in chapter 4.

Those new to statistics sometimes find its terminology difficult and it is important at this stage to be prepared to assimilate some new words and concepts. This may take a little time, but don't despair; every technical specialism from cookery to car repairs, from archaeology to avionics, has its own vocabulary, its 'jargon', and in most cases this is necessary in order to identify concepts, ideas or things which have no adequate definition in everyday speech. Apendix 2 on pp. 155–61 gives a glossary of all the major terms used in this book, as well as a glossary of the – limited – mathematical notation needed.

3.1 Variables, cases and values

In any study the researcher is concerned with a particular *population* or *universe*. Very occasionally, for example in the government's ten-yearly census, the population of the study coincides with the actual population of a country; normally, however, the term refers to a specific group of people, or institutions, or occurrences, about which the researcher wishes to make descriptive or analytic statements. For example, a population may be all the people arrested for arson in a particular year, or all the fatal accidents in the chemical industry in a specified period, or all the schools in one region. Within a population each individual unit is called a *case* or *observation*. A case is the basic unit of analysis. Most commonly in social science a case will be one person but, as the above examples suggest, it might also be an incident of some kind, or an organization. *The population, then, consists of all the available cases with which the study is concerned.*

Social scientists work with limited resources of time and money and therefore it is quite frequently impossible to study every single case in a population. Investigating the characteristics of all the schools in one particular town might be feasible, but collecting information about, say, all the schools in a county, or a region, may prove beyond the researcher's resources. In such cases we select a *sample* of cases to represent the population as a whole. These cases are selected either *randomly* (that is, so that each case in the population has an equal chance of being chosen for the sample) or according to some agreed strategy (e.g. one might want to be sure of including some very small schools in the sample, so the selection would be appropriately organized to ensure their selection). The sample cases then stand in place of the total universe of cases and it is the sample which we use as the basis for investigation. As we shall see later, sampling statistics are a distinctive field in their own right, and techniques have been developed to control and evaluate the selection of samples. Suffice to say here that the sample should be as representative as possible of the population from which it is drawn. (An extended discussion of sampling is provided in chapter 6. Sections 6.1, 6.2 and 6.3 can be read at this stage if further clarification is needed, but the statistical procedures involved in sampling – sections 6.5 onwards – demand an understanding of material in chapters 4 and 5.)

Having chosen our population of cases for study and, if necessary, having selected a sample from it, we must define the characteristics of the population in which we are interested. This, as was emphasized earlier, is a process of selection and definition guided by carefully considered theoretical analysis before beginning the study. No researcher is ever interested in every characteristic of a population, although some characteristics (such as age or gender) will be recorded in many studies. Each characteristic of a population is termed a *variable* because these are attributes which vary between cases. Any variable has a number of different possible *values* which may be simple categories (e.g. the variable 'gender' has two possible values, 'female' or 'male'), more complex descriptions (e.g. the different reasons given by criminals for committing an offence), or numerical values (e.g. a person's age, or the number of pupils in a school). Each case will have one – and only one – value for each variable.

A great deal of statistical analysis is now done using computer equipment of some kind and in order to utilize such equipment our information must be converted into 'machine-readable' form. In essence this means that all data must be presented in numerical form. Accordingly, an important stage of the research process is the allocation of a numerical value to each value of each variable for which we have information: this is called *coding*. Each value must have a code and each code must be unambiguous and must maintain the distinction between separate categories of each variable. A variable such as gender may be simply coded

Female 1
Male 2

but more complex variables with a greater number of categories will obviously require more codes, and variables with numeric values may take codes which are identical to the values themselves, e.g. the number of children in a family:

No children 0
One child 1
Two children 2
Three children 3

The very process of coding often forces the researcher to reconsider the categories selected for the variables in the sample, and a lot of minor coding decisions will nonetheless influence the final appearance of the data. In the example above, for instance, one could code each family size which occurs in the sample (even if there is only one family with, say, eight children) or limit the categories by using the same code for all families with four or more offspring. The former option will result in a proliferation of values with very few cases in each, and may clutter up later analysis; the latter will simplify the data but at the cost of sacrificing some detail.

One important guide to the way in which we categorize and code variables is the concept of *levels of measurement* or *scales*. There are three levels of measurement which are commonly identified and any variable can be defined according to its place on these scales. These levels are also important in helping us to determine which statistical procedures can be used with which variables, since many techniques are not universally applicable but depend, precisely, on the nature of the variable.

The three levels of measurement are:

3.1.1 Nominal scale

This can be defined as the simple classification of elements into useful categories. Variables measured on the nominal scale are essentially *qualitative* rather than *quantitative* in form, that is, the values are categories not numbers and cannot be ordered in any mathematically meaningful way. The most obvious example is that of 'gender'. Here there are two, and only two, possible values – male and female – and they are both simply equal and descriptive categories. A nominal level variable with only two possible values is referred to as a *dichotomous* variable. The number and type of values with other nominal level variables will depend on the study, but they all remain basically *names* for different possible elements of the variable. A single variable, 'religious belief', might have three possible values (Protestant Catholic, Other), or four (Protestant, Catholic, Jewish, Agnostic/Other), or more (Protestant, Catholic, Jewish, Muslim, Agnostic/Other), according to the population being studied and the particular interests of the researcher. Each value, however, remains just a descriptive category. When we come to code such categories for data analysis, the code numbers used also act just like names; they imply no particular order or relationship between the values. So,

Protestant	1
Catholic	2
Jewish	3
Agnostic/Other	4

is as valid as any completely different arrangement, e.g.

Agnostic/Other 0
Jewish 1
Protestant 2
Catholic 3

because the code numbers here are only the computer's name for the categories.

3.1.2 Ordinal scale

If the nominal level is the classification of elements into categories, then the ordinal level of measurement permits the ordering of those categories into a single rank or scale. This level applies to variables where we can distinguish between the values in terms of degree, but cannot measure the degree of difference between them. So, for example, a group of workers in an office rate their work environment on an ascending scale from 'Very poor' to 'Very good'. The scale might look like this:

Very poor 0
Poor 1
Satisfactory 2
Good 3
Very good 4

We know here that the rating 'Good' is better than the rating 'Poor', but we can't say how much better it is. We can assume that someone who responds with the rating 'Very poor' has a worse estimation of their work environment than the person whose response is 'Satisfactory', but we cannot measure the distance between those responses – one is simply higher, or lower, than the other. Notice, though, that when we assign code numbers to these ordered categories the codes can also express the rank order. So, here, the 'lowest' rating of the work environment gets the numerically lowest code (0) and so on, in ascending order to the highest estimation and the highest code number. What we must not do, however, is to treat the codes as values: we cannot say that, for instance, the code 4 is twice as great as code 2, only that 4 indicates a higher estimation than 2. Their only relationship therefore is one of *order*, not of *quantity*.

3.1.3 Interval scale

The interval scale implies both an ordering of categories and a measure of the difference between them. This, in turn, implies the existence of a common unit of standard measurement, by which the distance between values can be quantified. The values of an interval level variable will, therefore, be numerical values of some kind. The manager of a company may wish, for example, to record the number of absences each employee has had in one month and will produce a list of values like this:

No absences	0
One day's absence	1
Two days' absence	2
Three days' absence	3
Four days' absence	4
Five days' absence	5
Six days' absence	6

with six days being the greatest number of days' absence taken by any of his staff. Here we can see that not only do we have categories which are ordered (three days is more than one day but less than six days), but which are measured in a standard unit (number of days) which allows exact measurement (three days' absence is two days longer than one day but three days fewer than six days; four days' absence is twice as many as two days and so on). Note also that our code numbers can represent the values exactly, so that 'No absences' is represented by the code '0', 'One day' by the code '1': this allows us to treat the codes as real numbers and to manipulate them mathematically.

We can, then, think of the three[1] levels of measurement as an ascending scale of properties. A nominal level variable has simple properties defined in descriptive categories; an ordinal variable has descriptive categories that can be ordered on a scale; an interval variable has the properties of an ordinal one with the addition of a common unit of measurement by which we can quantify the difference between its values. These properties are also reflected in the meaning and use of the code numbers assigned to the values of each variable.

There is one further distinction to be made regarding the characteristics of variables, and this concerns the nature of the distribution of values. Essentially there are two categories.

3.1.4 Discrete variables

These are variables for which the values are limited to certain, countable categories. That is, not all values are possible, and the categories in which the values are defined cannot logically be subdivided. The number of children in a family, for instance, would be discrete because families can only have zero, one, two, three, four children, not 0.8 or 3.7 children. So units such as people, households, firms, towns and so on will always be discrete. Also, inevitably, all nominal variables are discrete because their values are purely descriptive categories and can therefore not be divided into smaller units.

3.1.5 Continuous variables

In contrast, continuous variables are those for which all values are theoretically possible, but the actual categories of which depend on the accuracy of measurement used. The variable 'time spent watching television' (e.g. in a survey of viewing habits) could, in principle, be measured in hours, minutes, seconds, or fractions of a second, the choice being entirely at the discretion of the researcher. Most continuous variables are, as one would imagine, interval level variables in which quantities of a particular element (e.g. time, age, distance etc.) are measured in a standard unit (hours, years, miles).

3.2 Variables and statistical analysis

It is not immediately obvious why we should wish to distinguish variables and their values in terms of their level of measurement. The reason lies in the problems faced when dealing with very different kinds of data, some of it consisting of simple description (e.g. age, gender, place of residence), some involving more complex concepts (e.g. a respondent's estimation of work satisfaction, or a doctor's definition of mental illness), and others requiring substantial numerical information (e.g. the number of houses built by successive councils). We cannot treat these different variables indiscriminately: each must be approached in a way which is likely to produce the most interesting and reliable analysis for that particular variable. It would be futile, for example, to try to add together definitions of mental illness in order to attempt to produce an 'average' definition, just as it would be wasteful if we did not try to use averages, proportions or ratios to analyse the fluctuations in council house building. Our awareness of the nature of variables, through concepts such as levels of measurement, enables us to use appropriate forms of analysis.

Three specific points can help to emphasize this.

1 The level of measurement is tied to the mode of analysis. Quite simply, certain techniques cannot be used with variables at certain levels. Using inapplicable statistical procedures renders the data at best meaningless, and at worst potentially misleading.

2 Coding can disguise the vital differences between variables. When we allocate a number to each value of a variable we render all variables similar in their statistical appearance. There may also be a temptation to treat the values numerically even if the codes actually stand not for real numbers but for descriptive categories. The relation between category and code depends on the nature of the variables and that is defined in the level of measurement. Also, using codes that are ambiguous or inadequate for the character of the data might result in loss of accuracy or misinterpretation.

3 If we are comparing variables, especially if we are in the first instance comparing them statistically using their codes, then we must be comparing like with like. Variables at different levels may need different interpretations, and some may not be compatible in statistical procedures.

To summarize, then, in Blalock's words: 'It is impossible to overemphasize the important point that, in using statistical techniques, one must be aware of the underlying assumptions that the procedure requires.'[2]

3.3 Some important qualifications

In practice these distinctions between variables can tend to become slightly blurred. In such instances we need to be even more conscious of the true nature of the data. Three common qualifications to these distinctions should be noted.

(1) *Coding.* Although we recognize the distinction between discrete and continuous variables, all variables are discrete inasmuch as

we have to opt for particular units of measurement and distinguish categories on that basis. It is not possible to code a genuine continuum so categories must be determined at some point by a decision about the accuracy of measurement required.

(2) *Grouped data*. For convenience it is sometimes useful to treat interval level data as ordinal data by aggregating information into larger categories. Take, for example, the variable 'age'. In the database which we will be using in the examples in this book (see Appendix 1), there is a substantial variation of responses within the probable range 16 years to 65 years old. The original responses are interval level data in the following form:

Respondent no.	Respondent's age
1	16
2	22
3	18
4	17
5	19
etc.	

In this form the information fulfils all the definitions of interval level data being numerical, measured in a standard unit (years), quantifiable and statistically manipulable. The researcher could use these data to produce summary statistics (e.g. averages, percentages etc.) or in more complex analysis with other interval level data. However, the researcher may also want to represent the data in a simple graphical or tabular form. For this purpose the number of values occurring may be far too large: a table showing all the ages that occurred (many of which may only have occurred once or twice) would not have much impact and would not represent the age pattern of the employees very clearly. The solution is to *aggregate* or *group* the data into ordered categories.

Respondent's age	No. of cases (i.e. number of respondents in category
16 years – 20 years	47
21 years – 30 years	95
31 years – 40 years	67
41 years – 50 years	71
51 years – 60 years	68
over 60 years	9
	–––
	357

Here we have all the information presented in a simple form by the device of grouping ages into logical categories. It is important to remember, nevertheless, that such aggregation, although useful, does simplify the data and, by making it in effect ordinal rather than interval, limits the statistical analysis available. Consequently, grouping should take place *after* initial analysis rather than before producing the data. The general rule is to measure and categorize at the highest level possible so that your original 'raw' data can later be aggregated if – but only if – it seems valuable to do so.

(3) *Summary measures*. When a body of data needs to be summarised in a single statistic, such as an *average*, then it can be useful to reverse normal procedure and treat a discrete variable as though it were continuous. For example, it is not uncommon to see figures such as the average number of children in a family presented in this way (e.g. 2.4 children). What it is important to remember is that *this is only a summary figure*: the number 2.4 has no logical, social meaning and could not have appeared as a response to an interviewer's question.

3.4 Descriptive, inductive and multivariate statistics

Statistical procedures are conventionally divided into three major categories, each of which corresponds to a specific group of techniques which fulfil a similar function. The categories are not, one should note, mutually exclusive: some techniques are relevant to more than one category. The distinction is more one of what we want to do with the techniques than of which techniques we employ.

3.4.1 Descriptive statistics

These are techniques which enable us to undertake the first task to analysis, the measuring, ordering and summarizing of data. As the name suggests, they are basically used to describe the characteristics of a sample or population in terms of one variable. Take the example used in 3.3 above: here we could say of our 357 employees that a) the most common age group was between 21 and 30; b) 47 of the 357 workers (13% per cent were aged 20 or under; c) (by adding all the ages and dividing by 357) the average age was 37. These are descriptive statistics – simple statements which describe the shape of the data and present the information about one variable in readily understandable figures. Because they are used in relation to only one variable at a time they are sometimes referred to as *univariate* statistics.

3.4.2 Inductive statistics

Near the beginning of this chapter I mentioned the distinction between *population* (all the cases in which we are interested) and a *sample* (a selection of cases taken to represent a population), saying that we often have to base our conclusions about the former on the more limited evidence of the latter. When we do this we are said to be *inducing* or *inferring* the characteristics of the population from the characteristics of the sample. The purpose of inductive statistics is to assist the researcher in the production of a representative sample and to enable the researcher to assess *how* representative a sample is. If, for example, our employees already referred to constitute a sample from a much larger workforce of, say, 2,000, then we would want to know not only how representative or 'typical' of the total workforce our 357 were, but also how close a statistic such as average age might be to the average age of the whole workforce. We would use inductive techniques to answer such questions. Inductive statistics are also commonly called *inferential* statistics.

3.4.3 Multivariate statistics

In the processes of induction and description our concern is with the details of one variable at any one time. Most social scientific enquiries are concerned not just with description (although this is an important first step), but with the relationship between variables. The establishment of a relationship is one of the most common exercises in social science. We very frequently use statistical techniques to identify and measure the connection between one variable and another. Such techniques are called *bivariate* (two variables) or *multivariate* ('many' variables) statistics. To explain their function more fully requires a brief look at a model of social research.

3.5 Variables and hypotheses

In chapter 2 the role of theory in the planning and interpretation of statistical research was emphasized, and it was suggested that the production of quantitative data is heavily dependent for its meaning and value on the quality of conceptual preparation in the early stages of research. It is not surprising, then, that the conventional model of social investigation begins with the formation of a *hypothesis*, that is a statement about the relation between two or more variables which can be empirically tested. Note the difference here between theory and hypothesis: the latter will be derived from the former but will be stated in such a way that it can be used as the basis for the research process itself.

Let us take a simple example involving, initially, just two variables. Emile Durkheim in his famous study, *Suicide*, developed a theory of suicide which focussed not on the individual but on the rate of suicide in a nation as a whole. In doing so he produced a number of arguments at the theoretical level concerning the factors determining the suicide rate, some of which related to the stability or instability of a country's economy. A typical hypothesis derived from this theory was that a rise in the number of recorded bankruptcies in a country would result in a rise in the number of recorded suicides. We are dealing with two variables here, the 'bankruptcy rate' and the 'suicide rate'. We refer to these as the *independent* and the *dependent* variables. The hypothesis is normally in the form of an assertion that a change in the independent variable (bankruptcy) will result in a change in the dependent variable (suicide). The independent variable is, consequently, sometimes referred to as the *explanatory* variable: its variation explains the variation in the dependent variable (for an extended discussion see section 7.1).

(1) The time sequence must be clear. In other words, it must be evident that the change in the dependent variable occurred *after* the change in the independent variable: it is obviously not sufficient simply to observe that both changed without un-equivocally identifying the sequence.

(2) Any other possible factors that might be causing the change in the dependent variable must be eliminated. A third variable may in fact be decisive but not, at first, evident. For example, the extent of poverty might be the main cause of increasing suicides:

poverty would then be an *intervening* variable between bankruptcy and suicide. So, an increase in the rate of bankrupties
might be producing an increase in poverty which, in turn,
produces an increase in the suicide rate. The crucial point here is
that if the bankruptcy rate did not change but (for some other
reason) poverty increased, then the suicide rate would also
increase and our hypothesis about bankruptcy and suicide would
no longer be acceptable. The relation between variables in social
science is often complex and I shall consider some more
refinements on this theme in chapter 8.

(3) It must be clear that the relationship between the variables
hasn't occurred purely by chance. The size of the change in each
variable and the *association* between those changes may be a result
of the particular sample that has been chosen, or may not, in fact,
be attributable to anything more than random fluctuations in the
respective rates. This is where multivariate statistics are particularly useful. They give the researcher an indication of the
probability that the association under scrutiny happened by
chance or the likelihood of it demonstrating the effect of one
variable on another. These statistics can also help the researcher
to gauge the *strength* of the association (i.e. how much of the
change in the dependent variable is due to the change in the
independent) and its *direction* (i.e. have we correctly identified
which is the independent variable and which the dependent?).

3.6 A word of caution

In chapters 1 and 2 the shortcomings and criticisms of the 'positivist'
model of social science, with its reliance on the natural sciences as
the model for social enquiry, were discussed. It is worth repeating
here that the social analyst can never treat the objects of a study as
inanimate and asocial. Even when, as in the example above, we are
dealing with statistical information such as rates, we have to
remember that these rates are socially produced: they are the
outcome of people making decisions, classifying behaviour, impos-
ing definitions and selecting information to present. There are two
important considerations which derive from this

(1) The relationships which we observe and statistically establish,
should always be regarded as *associations* between variables, and
not as simple *causal* relations. The nature of social behaviour

means that relations will rarely, if ever, be uncomplicated, one-way relations between two factors: other variables will always impinge and influence; the variation in one factor may be attributable to variation in two, three or more other variables, all of which are themselves related. This is why we tend not to speak of causality but of association, not of determination but of probability in relationships.

(2) This reasonable caution which all social scientists must observe also affects our model of research procedure. This model is derived primarily from natural science procedure and needs to be treated as a model rather than as a description of the reality of a research process. As indicated in chapter 2, the normal research project takes a much more complex course, requiring as it may the rethinking or refinement of hypotheses in the light of initial research findings, the discovery of completely new lines of investigation, and the unavoidable modification of the research model to fit the constraints of the research situation. A heartening trend in recent years has been the tendency of sociologists to describe how their research was actually carried out, and how the constraints involved in this effected their findings.[3]

Summary

The social scientist sets out to study certain characteristics (*variables*) of a particular *population* of *cases*. Constrained by time, money and geographical location, the researcher selects a *sample* of cases from the population, utilizing statistical procedures to ensure the representativeness of the sample. A number of *hypotheses* have been framed concerning the major variables of the study and data are produced through documentary analysis, questionnaire surveys and personal interviews in order to assess these hypotheses. In the process of the research certain assumptions have to be revised and some lines of enquiry abandoned due to the difficulty of producing adequate data: the researcher finds certain variables to be rather more significant than was at first thought.

Initially, the researcher uses *descriptive statistics* to produce an ordered summary of the information produced in the study. This process also enables the researcher to evaluate more closely the relative importance of certain variables and to consider the direction of further analysis. *Multivariate* statistics are then employed to explore the relationships between variables, the procedures becom-

ing more complex as a number of statistically supportable statements, related to the original hypotheses, and constituting, perhaps,
a theoretical reassessment of the topic of the study.

Finally, the researcher will want to utilize *visual representation* –
graphs, charts and tables – in order to present the findings of the
study to other people in a way that is both comprehensible and
permits evaluation of the methods and conclusions of the study.

In chapter 4 some *descriptive statistics* used in the ordering of data
will be considered and we shall encounter the research data which
are going to serve as the raw material for our analysis.

Further exercises

A Using either the full database (357 cases) or the database sample (89
cases) *create a file* on your computer consisting of the data. You should
learn the correct procedure for data entry and for the addition, correction
and deletion of information. This should also help to clarify the meanings
of the concepts of case, variable and value.

B When all the information has been accurately entered, *save the file* for
future use. On a microcomputer this will normally be done on a *floppy
disk*. You should now have a permanent copy of the data which you can
'access' (call up) whenever you want to undertake statistical procedures.

Notes

1 There is a fourth level of measurement sometimes used, the *ratio* level.
  This differs from the interval level only in that the scale has an identifiable
  zero point. However, most social science variables at the interval level do,
  at least theoretically, have a zero point so that we shall, for the purposes
  of this book, overlook the interval/ratio distinction.
2 H.M. Blalock, *Social Statistics* (2nd edn, New York, McGraw-Hill, 1972).
3 An excellent and enlightening example is C. Bell and H. Newby (eds),
  Sociological Research (London, Allen and Unwin, 1977).

4 Ordering the Data: Frequency Distribution and Visual Representation

The first task of statistical analysis in the treatment of 'raw' (i.e. unprocessed) data is that of translating them into a form which can be readily understood and reliably used, both by the 'consumer' and by the researcher in the process of further analysis or explanation. Most social scientific data start life in the form of individual pieces of information collected together with the purpose of producing a picture of a social group. So, for example, a researcher interested in the social background of company directors in certain major companies will have to begin by discovering the background of each individual director; but these data will soon be translated into generalizations about the collectivity. The researcher will show the number of directors who went to a state or a private school, the proportion who are married, the occupations most commonly held by their parents. The individual pieces of information will be combined into categories, grouped, described and compared. In this chapter we shall look at one fairly simple set of data to see how this process is undertaken.

4.1 From raw data to frequency distribution

The example we are going to use is a single variable drawn from a study of office workers in local government. The variable is 'length of service in the present organization' or 'service' for short. This is a fairly typical variable providing background information on the employees in a study of occupation and organization. It was also, in this case, a fairly important variable because the researchers were interested in the career patterns of employees. The data were taken from computerized personnel records held by the employer (but *with* the consent of the employees and their union representative) and the process consisted simply of calculating the length of service from the date at which each individual began employment, and recording this in terms of years and months. At this stage the data are:

(a) 'raw': that is, they have not been processed or ordered in any way
(b) based solely on the individual employee
(c) recorded at *interval level* (i.e. length of service is in years and could be treated mathematically)

As such, however, they are of little or no analytical use to the researcher – they are 357 individual pieces of information. (See Appendix 1: in this Appendix the database is presented as a list of 357 cases, each with a value for each of the four variables, *age, service, grade, gender*. This represents the initial form in which these data were collected and organized prior to any other processing.) The researcher may be able to ascertain the shortest serving employee and the longest serving employee; it may be possible to discern, very approximately, which periods of employment occur most frequently. Beyond that, nothing can be done without some reorganization of the data.

The initial ordering of data is done by the construction of a *frequency distribution*: this simply shows the frequency with which (i.e. how many times) each value occurs. This can be represented by two columns, one listing every value of the variable that occurs, the other showing the number of cases which take that value.

Table 4.1 shows a frequency distribution for the variable *service*, as printed out by the computer program FREQUENCIES which is part of SPSS (Statistical Package for the Social Sciences), the most widely used set of statistical programs for computer analysis of sociological data. The sum of the frequencies column is then, of course, the number of cases in the sample. This, however, still looks very cumbersome and, with a relatively large number of cases, there remain many values with relatively small frequencies. The normal practice in such a situation would be to construct a smaller number of larger categories by joining together groups of adjacent values. Indeed, one of the important elements in categorizing data is to make absolutely clear which cases are included in which categories. Table 4.2 shows a frequency distribution of this variable produced by the computer program SPSS, after the categories have been grouped.

Table 4.1 *Frequency distribution for the variable service*

Service

Code	Freq	Adj PCT	Cum PCT	Code	Freq	Adj PCT	Cum PCT	Code	Freq	Adj PCT	Cum PCT
0	42	12	12	12	6	2	85	24	5	1	96
1	44	12	24	13	5	1	86	26	1	0	96
2	16	4	29	14	6	2	88	27	2	1	97
3	15	4	33	15	2	1	89	28	1	0	97
4	46	13	46	16	2	1	89	29	1	0	97
5	49	14	59	17	2	1	90	31	2	1	98
6	15	4	64	18	2	1	90	34	2	1	99
7	26	7	71	19	3	1	91	35	1	0	99
8	14	4	75	20	6	2	93	38	2	1	99
9	10	3	78	21	3	1	94	39	2	1	100
10	13	4	81	22	2	1	94				
11	7	2	83	23	2	1	95				

There are a number of points to consider regarding this table:

1 The breadth or *interval* of each category is not equal. It is preferable to produce categories with equal intervals (e.g. five years each) but to have done that here would either have produced exceptionally large categories (meaning a further loss of detail) or, if much smaller intervals had been chosen, would again have left us with a large number of categories containing relatively small frequencies.

2 The boundaries of each category are unambiguously stated. The first category includes every employee with anything less than a full year's service; the second category includes all those with one year's service but less than a full two years', and so on.

3 Note that each category has been given a code number for entry into the computer.

Constructing a frequency distribution, therefore, is simply a matter of counting cases to establish how the cases are distributed, or spread, across the range of occurring values. A frequency distribution organizes the information into a more readable and comprehensible form; it enables the researcher to identify any significant patterns in the distribution of cases; it provides 'leads' for further investigation. The simplest form of frequency distribution is a list of all the values that occur, and their respective frequencies; if these values are grouped into categories then we must be aware that the choice of categories, their number and interval size, will in itself impose some pattern on the data.

We can now tell from our frequency distribution that, for example, 42 of our 357 employees had been with the organization for less than a year; or that, in contrast, 32 had been there for twenty years or more. The next step is to convert such *proportions* into a more commonly used form, that of *percentages*. The column headed RELATIVE FREQ (PCT) in our computer printout in table 4.2 shows the number of cases in each category converted to a percentage of the total number of cases. Mathematically this is, of course, simply done by dividing the number in any one category by the total number of cases and then multiplying by 100. Thus,

$$\frac{42}{357} = 0.1176 \times 100 = 11.8\% \text{ (rounded up)}$$

Converting to a percentage has two great advantages:

1 It translates the proportions into a more easily understood form, e.g. it is now clear that the largest category, that of employees with four or more, but less than six years' service, constitutes just over one-quarter of all the cases.

2 It standardizes the data so that they can be compared with other similar information. The comparison of two samples cannot be done solely with absolute frequencies as these are affected by the overall size of the sample; percentages provide a common form of measurement. To compare, for instance, 95 cases in a

Table 4.2 *Grouped frequency distribution for the variable service*

Service group

Category label	Code	Absolute Freq	Relative Freq (PCT)	Adjusted Freq (PCT)	Cum Freq (PCT)
Up to 1 year	0	42	11.8	11.6	11.8
1 yr up to 2 yrs	1	44	12.3	12.3	24.1
2 yrs up to 4 yrs	2	31	8.7	8.7	32.8
4 yrs up to 6 yrs	3	95	26.6	26.6	59.4
6 yrs up to 10 yrs	4	65	18.2	18.2	77.6
10 yrs up to 15 yrs	5	37	10.4	10.4	88.0
15 yrs up to 20 yrs	6	11	3.1	3.1	91.0
20 years and more	7	32	9.0	9.0	100.0
	Total	357	100.0	100.0	

sample of 357 with the same number of cases in a sample of 200 would require just such standardization; the frequencies are the same but represent, respectively, 27 per cent and 48 per cent of their samples.

There are in table 4.2 three columns of percentage frequencies. The first, as we have seen, gives the *relative* frequency, the percentage of cases in each category; the second is an *adjusted* frequency, in which the computer recalculates the percentages, ignoring any missing cases. This is a useful facility in instances where the proportion of missing cases may distort the distribution. The third column shows us the *cumulative* frequency; as the name suggests, this is calculated by adding each category's frequency to the preceding one, and can be done with the absolute frequency as well as the percentage figures. The usefulness of the cumulative frequency is that it provides an instant indication of how many cases lie above or below a particular value. Here, for instance, we can see that approximately 33 per cent of the cases were to be found in the first three categories – in other words, one-third of the employees had less than four years' service. However, almost two-thirds of all the employees (60 per cent) had less than six years' service, i.e. were included in one of the first four categories. Such statements not only provide useful descriptive generalizations about the distribution, but also draw our attention to potentially significant patterns. Here, for example, the researcher would be interested in the concentration of cases in category 4.

One more descriptive statistic commonly used with frequency distributions might usefully be mentioned here and that is the ratio. This expresses a relative frequency in the same way as a proportion or a percentage but it does so by comparing any one category *either* to the total number of cases *or* to any one (or more) category. For example, the ratio of all employees to employees with between ten and 15 years' service (category 5) is 357:37, or approximately, 10:1; the ratio of employees with four or more years' service to those with less than four years' service is 240:117 or, approximately, 2:1. It is common to reduce ratios to the form n:1 (where n denotes whichever number is appropriate), but not essential. It is, however, important to distinguish clearly which categories are being compared, and especially whether one category is being compared to the total number of cases, or to one or more other categories only. The difference is obviously crucial, as can be shown using the first example above in three different ratios.

1 The ratio of *all employees* to those in category 5 = 357:37 = 9.6:1 (another way of seeing this would be to say that approximately 1 in 10 of all employees in the study had been with the organization between ten and 15 years).

2 The ratio of employees in all *other* categories to those in category 5 = 320:37 = 8.6:1 (this is to say, for every employee in category 5 there are about nine employees with a different length of service).

3 The ratio of employees with less than ten years' service to those with ten to (but less than) 15 years' service = 277:37 = 7.5:1 (which is to say, for every employee with at least ten but less than 15 years' service, there are almost eight employees with less service).

Simple frequency distributions, both relative and cumulative, proportions, percentages and ratios are easy-to-use statistics which permit us to make initial observations about the data, to identify areas of interest and to guide further analysis. In order to reach this first stage of analysis, however, we have had to group the data into categories and to produce figures which summarize the absolute and relative size of these categories. The data are now:

(a) 'processed': they have been ordered and simplified
(b) based on groups of cases, not on individuals
(c) represented at ordinal level (ranked categories)

In achieving this management of the data we have, unavoidably, lost some information, some individual detail, and have imposed upon the data a set of categories which arise partly from the researcher's interpretation of the distribution of the cases, and partly from the constraints created by the need for comprehension and generalization. It is this latter need which also governs the transformation of numerical data into visual images and symbols, the subject to which we turn in section 4.3 below. Before we do so we need to look at an important extension of the *ratio*, the concept of a *rate*.

4.2 The concept of a rate

The ratio can be extended into the concept of the rate. This is so commonly used, and almost certainly misused, that it deserves separate attention. Like a ratio, a rate is a comparison of two figures, but not of two values within the same variable. It is the measurement of the frequency with which a value occurs compared to the frequency with which it could occur. Commonly it is used to express the frequency of an occurrence for a particular population: the unemployment rate, for example, is the number of people recorded as unemployed compared to the potential working population of the country. The suicide rate is the number of deaths recorded as suicide compared to all recorded deaths. Ott, Larson and Mendenhall[1] define a rate as:

$$\frac{\text{number of actual occurrences}}{\text{number of possible occurrences}} \quad \text{(divided by)}$$

This means that a rate is expressed differently from a ratio. For the latter we write that, in a particular town, the ratio of unemployed people to employed people was 1:10; for the former we would write that the unemployment rate was .1 or, more commonly, 10 per cent.

Because they represent useful summary measures of frequency, rates are very often used to compare similar variables in different populations or the same variable measured over time. An example of the first would be a comparison of unemployment rates for six towns in the same month; an example of the second would be a comparison of the monthly unemployment rate in the same town over six consecutive months. In both cases the rate allows one to *standardize* otherwise very different figures in order to make a comparison. However, we have to be careful with rates, especially to make sure that the definition, recording and measurement of a variable has been undertaken in the same way in each of the populations being compared.

Let us say, for example, that we wish to compare the rate of female employment in our clerical workers' case study with other groups of workers. In our study the ratio of women to the total number of employees is 173:357; that is, the rate of female employment is 48 per cent. In a second company there are 68 women workers out of a workforce of 118: a rate of 58 per cent; in a third company there are 245 women workers out of a workforce of 782: a rate of 31 per cent. The rate enables us to compare directly figures of a different magnitude. Here, the rate is little different from a ratio or simple percentage, however comparisons over time allow us to be slightly more sophisticated. It is uncommon for the social

Table 4.3 Union membership and density rates, selected years, 1911–79

	Manual			White-collar			White-collar union density (%) / Manual union density (%)
	Union membership (000s)	Potential union membership (000s)	Union density (%)	Union membership (000s)	Potential union membership (000s)	Union density (%)	
1911	2,730.9	13,141	20.8	398.3	3,297	12.1	58.2
1920	7,124.1	13,271	53.7	1,129.2	3,847	29.4	54.7
1931	3,544.0	14,157	25.0	1,025.4	4,639	22.1	88.4
1948	7,055.7	14,027	50.3	2,062.1	6,243	33.0	65.6
1968	6,636.9	13,322	49.8	3,056.0	9,381	32.6	65.5
1970	7,095.0	12,852	55.2	3,533.0	9,688	36.5	66.1
1973	6,968.9	12,468	55.9	3,966.3	10,266	38.6	69.1
1974	7,082.3	12,362	57.3	4,130.8	10,458	39.5	68.9
1975	7,112.1	12,327	57.7	4,488.8	10,715	41.9	72.6
1976	7,321.6	12,322	59.4	4,632.3	11,004	42.1	70.9
1977	7,445.3	12,265	60.7	4,837.9	11,251	43.0	70.8
1978	7,549.7	12,168	62.0	5,029.1	11,467	43.9	70.8
1979	7,577.5	12,035	63.0	5,124.7	11,652	44.0	69.8

Source: Bain and Price (1983)

Note: The following occupational groups have been defined as white-collar: foremen, overlookers, and supervisors; scientists, technologists and technicians; clerical and administrative workers; security personnel, including the police; professional workers; salesmen, shop assistants, commercial travellers; government administrators and executive officials; and 'creative' occupations such as artists, musicians and entertainers.

researcher to be able to make comparisons over time using original data generated by research: most studies take place over, and thus refer to, a specific and limited time period. Similar studies of the same population taken at different times are rarely identical and commonly present problems of comparison, unless originally planned as a comparative series. Studies are hard to replicate because populations alter, and conditions of research alter: it is extremely difficult to retain consistency and continuity in certain variables while studying change in others. Consequently, most time comparisons of rates are made using data produced through standard, regular government studies.

Table 4.3 shows figures for the number of employees belonging to trade unions in the years between 1911 and 1979 (the highest point of union membership this century). The table is divided into manual and white-collar unions and, for each of these, there are three columns of information. The first column gives the actual membership for each year (in thousands); the second column gives the potential membership – that is, the number of manual workers in the labour force available for recruitment into trades unions; the third column gives what is called *union density* and which is, in fact, a *rate* of unionization. Density is measured by dividing column 1 by column 2 and multiplying the result by 100 to produce a percentage figure. By looking carefully at a few examples from these figures it is possible to appreciate the usefulness of the rate.

The importance of the rate is that it standardizes figures of different magnitudes and enables us to interpret changes in absolute numbers which might otherwise be deceptive. A number of examples will illustrate this:

(1) *Standardization*. If, for example, we wish to compare union membership of manual and white-collar unions in 1931 it is difficult to do so on the absolute figures. There were clearly more manual trades unionists (three and a half million compared to just over a million white-collar), but there were also many more manual workers (and thus potential members). By calculating the rate the two sets of figures can be compared, and we find that, in fact, the density of each group was not so different: 25 per cent and 22 per cent.

(2) *Deceptive numbers*. The figures for manual union membership reveal a fall in membership from 1970 to 1973 of 127,000. However, at the same time the potential membership also fell. Calculation of the rate reveals that the actual density of

membership increased slightly. The opposite can be observed in the white-collar figures for the period 1948-68. Total membership shows a spectacular rise from two to three million members. Yet calculation of the rate shows that even this increase did not keep pace with the increased number of white-collar workers in the labour force: density actually fell slightly.

(3) *Percentage change.* Sometimes we wish to express the rise and fall of a social phenomenon in terms of a percentage change. Again, the rate can be most useful. Sometimes the change in the rate expresses the change in numbers. The number of manual workers in trade unions doubled, for example, between 1931 and 1948; the manual labour force remained fairly stable and, consequently, the rate of membership also doubled. Note, however, that we must be careful how we express the percentage change. It is correct to say, in this case, that the rate of membership increased from 25 per cent (1931) to 50 per cent (1948), an increase in density of 25 per cent. However, the 1948 figure is, in fact, double that of the earlier figures so the increase of one over the other is 100 per cent. It is important to distinguish these two measurements: a rise of 25 per cent on a figure of 25 per cent is 100 per cent increase; a rise of 25 per cent on a figure of 50 per cent is a 50 per cent increase. For example, the density of white-collar membership doubled between 1931 and 1979 but this was an increase in density of 22 per cent, and it represented an increase in actual membership of 400 per cent (one million to over five million).

(4) *Further calculations.* The standardizing effect of the rate allows us not only to compare quite different sets of figures but also to compare rates themselves. The final column in table 4.3 shows a third rate calculated from the other two. This is a figure which shows the relative size of the two density rates. It is calculated by dividing the white-collar union density by the manual union density and multiplying by 100. So, in 1920, for instance the density of white-collar unionization was only 54 per cent of manual unionization. By the end of the period (1979) this had risen to almost 70 per cent. This, then, is a relative rate of union density, produced by dividing one rate into another.

There is one further way of utilizing rates and that is in the construction of *index numbers*. Index numbers are used in the comparison of rates, especially using the rate for one year as the *base* or measure for all other years. To illustrate this from table 4.3: if we take the first year of our period as the *base year*, then we call the density figure for that year (12.1 per cent) 100. Each subsequent year's rate is then calculated as a proportion of 100 by dividing each year by the base year and multiplying by 100. So, for example, for 1920:

$$\frac{29.4}{12.1} = 2.429 \times 100 = 242.9 = 243 \text{ (rounded up)}$$

Table 4.4 shows the index numbers calculated for white-collar membership density (column 1). The advantage of index numbers as a way of expressing the rate is twofold: firstly, it expresses the proportional rise or fall in a rate from one year to another; secondly, it relates all the figures to a single year for standard comparison. We do not, of course, have to take the first year as our base. We might choose to take another important year – 1948, for instance, as the first post-war figure available. Column 2 of table 4.4 shows the index numbers recalculated using 1948 as the base year. As is obvious, a change in the base year can effect an important change in the appearance of the statistics, and interpreting a table of index numbers always requires care with respect to how the index numbers have been organized.

Table 4.4   *White-collar union density represented as an index using two different base years*

	1	2	
1911	100	37	
1920	243	89	
1931	187	67	
1948	273	100	
1968	269	99	
1970	302	111	(All figures rounded to the
1973	319	117	nearest whole number)
1974	326	120	
1975	346	127	
1976	348	128	
1977	355	130	
1978	363	133	
1979	364	133	
	(Base = 1911)	(Base = 1948)	

The rate, then, is a very valuable descriptive statistic but one which must be used with care: it is wise to bear in mind that it should, wherever possible, be used together with the actual figures for which it was produced.

4.3 Visual representation of frequency distributions

The producer or analyst of numerical data commonly has to present information in a form which is readily understandable to the 'lay person' and which accurately but clearly represents or summarizes interesting elements of the data. A popular solution to this problem is the use of visual representation: charts, diagrams, tables and other devices. Used honestly and sensibly these can be of great value but, like other statistical techniques, they are open to abuse. It is important to learn how to produce visual representations properly as this will also prepare you to assess the reliability of visual techniques used by others.

The basis of the frequency distribution was simply that of *counting cases*, and the simplest pictorial version of a frequency distribution is really no more than that either. Figure 4.1 shows the form in which a number of computer programs (this one happens to be SPSS) produce a basic *histogram*. Each case is represented by a dot or asterisk and arranged horizontally across the page with the values or

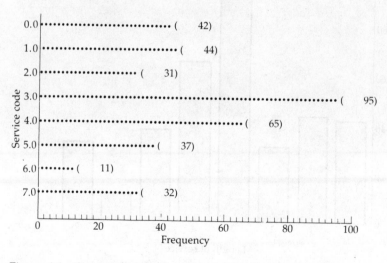

Figure 4.1 *Simple histogram for the variable service (grouped data).*

categories listed vertically, a format similar to that of the frequency distribution in table 4.2. The individual dots could be joined into continuous lines, in which case the figure is called a *line histogram*. Crude as they may be, the advantage of such figures is that they provide an overall impression of the relative dimensions of each category.

The most common form of histogram, however, represents quantities not as asterisks or lines but as blocks or bars. Figure 4.2 shows the same frequency distribution represented by bars set on two axes. The horizontal (x) axis shows the category which each bar represents while the vertical (y) axis indicates the number of cases in each category. Such histograms are sometimes referred to as *bar charts* although, strictly, a bar chart is a histogram in which the categories are of equal size. This is of some importance in the impression conveyed by such a figure: the relative frequency for each category is represented not just by the height of each bar (although this is what we primarily notice) but also by the bar's *area*. To be truly accurate the area of each bar should be proportional to the number of cases represented. In other words the distance between the beginning of one category and the beginning of the next one (called the *class interval*) should be equal and constant. In this example, this would mean, for instance, categories of a standard

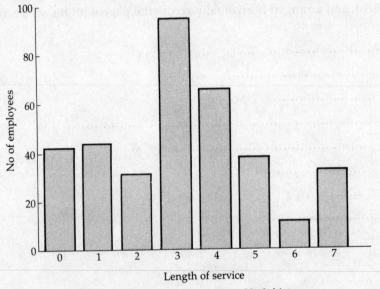

Figure 4.2 *The variable service represented as a block histogram*

number of years. In such a true *bar chart* the area of each bar is proportional to the frequency represented. It should be noted, however, that the selection of equal categories does not necessarily reveal more about the data.

Occasionally we might choose to emphasize the rise and fall of a distribution by representing it on a single line. This is achieved by drawing a line which joins the midpoints of each bar and is called a *frequency polygon* or *line chart*. Figure 4.3 shows a frequency polygon based upon the block histogram from figure 4.2. It is extremely important to remember that this is only a representational device: it is not a graph, and *values cannot be read off from any point on the line*. With all such grouped distributions we are dealing with discrete variables and each bar, or its midpoint, must be treated as a separate category not as a point on a continuous line of values.

One other form of bar chart can be used without axes: this is called a *compound* or *component* bar chart and takes the form of a single bar divided into sections representing the various categories. Sections will normally be coloured or shaded differently to distinguish them and the chart should be clearly labelled to indicate how many cases, or what percentage of the cases, each section

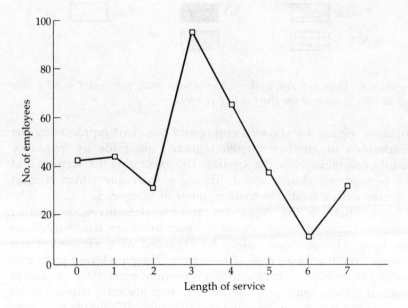

Figure 4.3 *Frequency polygon drawn from figure 4.2*

(a)

Grade Category label	Code	Absolute freq	Relative freq (PCT)	Adjusted freq (PCT)	Cum freq (PCT)
All clerical	1.	187	52.4	52.4	52.4
All APT	2.	81	22.7	22.7	75.1
SO	3.	26	7.3	7.3	82.4
PO+	4.	45	12.6	12.6	95.0
Other	5.	18	5.0	5.0	100.0
	Total	357	100.0	100.0	

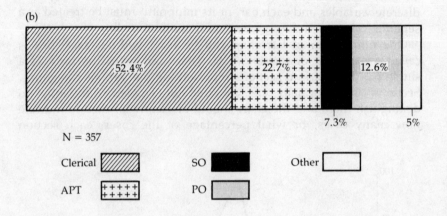

(b)

N = 357

Figure 4.4   *Frequency distribution of the variable grade represented as (a) a table and as (b) a compound bar chart (using percentages)*

contains. Figure 4.4 shows a compound bar chart representing the distribution of another variable, 'grade', alongside its frequency distribution table. Note the separate key explaining the sections and the percentages clearly stated. This is a technique which is most effective with a relatively small number of categories.

In addition to the histogram and its derivatives, two other common forms of simple visual representation are worth mentioning here. The *pictogram* might be regarded as a version of our original counting-cases type of histogram. Here a relevant picture or symbol represents each case, or a proportion, percentage or ratio of cases. It is most commonly used in the latter instance, where a small number of symbols can be employed to represent a simple ratio (e.g. n:1) of one value to another. An example from the data quoted above might be a comparison between the number of employees who had been with the organization for less than two years and the number who had been there for two years or more. The actual ratio here is 86:271 or 1:3.1. That is to say, for every new employee there were approximately three 'established' employees. Choosing appropriate symbols (I have chosen acorns and oak trees) a simple pictogram is drawn to express this ratio visually (figure 4.5a). It would also be possible to use the same symbol for both parts of the ratio, by making one symbol three times larger than the other. Here, however, we run into difficulties: a symbol three times larger in height and width will not be three times larger in *area*, but will, in fact, be nine (three squared) times larger than the original. Figure 4.5b illustrates this problem. This can be avoided by altering one dimension of the symbol only but this tends to produce an unattractive pictogram. If one does wish to utilize a single symbol (here one leaf will = one employee) then repetition is probably safer than enlargement (see figure 4.5c).

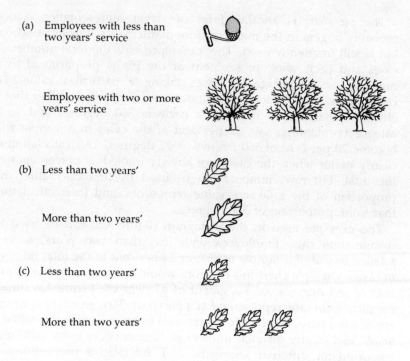

(a) Employees with less than two years' service

Employees with two or more years' service

(b) Less than two years'

More than two years'

(c) Less than two years'

More than two years'

Figure 4.5 *Pictograms of the ratio of 'new' to 'established' employees*

Grade

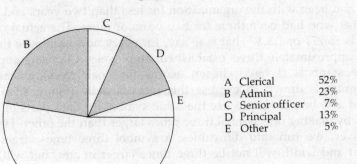

A	Clerical	52%
B	Admin	23%
C	Senior officer	7%
D	Principal	13%
E	Other	5%

Figure 4.6 *The variable grade represented as a pie chart (produced using the Statsease program on an Apple IIe)*

The *pie chart* is another form of visual representation which probably lingers in the memory from mathematics lessons at school but is still frequently used. The 'pie' represents the total number of cases and each 'slice' or segment of the pie is proportional to a number, or percentage, of cases taking a particular value. To calculate the size of each segment it is necessary to remember that a circle is measured in degrees (a circle is 360 degrees) and so a category containing, say, 20 per cent of the cases in a sample will become 20 per cent of 360 degrees = 72 degrees. This calculation is clearly easier when the cases are already quoted as percentages of the total, but raw numbers can be used by first calculating the proportion of the total *each* value represents, and then calculating that same proportion of 360 degrees.

The example used in the pictogram (figure 4.5) can be used to demonstrate this. Employees with less than two years' service totalled 86 out of a sample of 357, or 24 per cent of the total number of cases. On a pie chart this category would be represented as 24 per cent of 360 degrees, or a segment of 87 degrees. Figure 4.6 shows the pictogram ratio represented as a pie chart. Two words of warning are needed here. Firstly, pie charts tend to be most effective when a small, and clearly distinct, number of segments are used; labelling, colouring for different segments, and the relative proportions of each 'slice' become more difficult the greater the number of segments employed. Secondly, if more than one pie chart is being used, especially where different samples are being compared, then the size of the charts (and thus of their segments) must be kept in proportion. A segment which represents 24 per cent of a sample of 357 (n = 86) should not be drawn the same size as a segment representing 24 per cent of a sample of 80 cases (n = 19): this would be misleading. A sense of scale has to be observed.

4.4 Computer graphics, colour and three dimensions

Virtually every contemporary computer has the capability to produce pictures and diagrams to represent numerical information. This is normally referred to as the 'graphics capability' of a machine. Such techniques may be contained in a specialist graphics program, or incorporated in an appropriate program such as a statistics package. Their nature ranges from extreme simplicity to very considerable sophistication; at one level the printing of a row of asterisks to represent class in a frequency distribution; at another, the three-dimensional plotting of points on a graph or matrix for two or more variables. The social scientist will most frequently use the more simple graphics in the production of visual representations of data and, of the techniques mentioned so far, histograms, bar charts and pie charts are available fairly widely.

All the techniques considered in this chapter have been appropriate for one variable only (that is, they have been ways of representing the distribution of cases across the values of one variable), but there are, of course, also important methods of representing the relationship between two variables, the best-known being line graphs, which are discussed in chapter 7. It is important to note here, however, that much can be done to enhance the appearance of even the simplest diagram.

The first area of attention is the *labelling* of a diagram. This is of paramount importance as inaccurate or incomplete labelling renders any chart useless or, worse, misleading. Plenty of space and care should be given to the information provided beside a diagram: it is this that enables the reader to make proper sense of what you have drawn. Computer graphics procedures often provide a choice of size, style and position of written labels as well as offering the choice of full or abbreviated titles and variable or value names.

Many computer programs also offer *colour* variations, enabling the user to distinguish sections of a bar chart or pie chart by different colours rather than by simple shading or labelling. Although many printed media do not permit colour reproduction it can be a simple and valuable way of enhancing the production of a diagram, whether manually or by computer.

It is not uncommon to see univariate (single variable) charts, such as we have been considering, presented as *three-dimensional* pictures. Thus it is possible to turn the bars of a bar chart into tiny skyscrapers, and a pie chart into the end of a stick of rock, if you wish. Such techniques add visual appeal and variety to the otherwise rather 'flat' diagrams; they give the opportunity for incorporating more shading, colours, or even pictures, into the charts. However, the use of three dimensions to represent information which is fundamentally two-dimensional has its pitfalls. Firstly, it introduces what appears to be further information, but which may, in effect, be just decoration; secondly, it may distract the reader from the detail of the chart; thirdly, and most importantly, it can generate confusion over the accurate interpretation of the diagram, particularly with regard to which line, edge or point of a chart should be read against any accompanying scale. In short, one must be careful that any additions or embellishments to a chart assist, rather than obstruct, the reader's understanding.

4.5 Reading and interpreting statistical graphics

In this chapter the emphasis has been on the *production* of various common forms of visual representation but, in practice, most social scientists will spend more time interpreting the work produced by other people. A few words are therefore necessary on how to approach the analysis of such work. I have already mentioned some of the possible causes of misinterpretation and, in particular, the golden rule that all the information required to interpret the table should be clearly available. To simplify, the use of visual representation can be divided into three loose categories.

(1) *Illustrative.* The writer uses visual representation to illustrate a point of information already fully stated in the text. For example, it may be stated in the text that, in a particular study, the ratio of male office managers to female office managers was 10:1. A simple pictogram could accompany the text showing ten male figures to one female figure. The pictogram does not add any new

information, it simply expresses an established point in different, and perhaps more memorable, form.

(2) *Explanatory*. The writer provides some information in the text but extends this through the provision of visual representation. For example, it may be stated in the text that 70 per cent of these female managers had at least ten years' service with their company compared to only 30 per cent of male managers. Two pie charts are then provided, one for male and one for female managers, showing the proportion of each group with different lengths of service. Here the main point stressed by the writer is illustrated but, in addition, complementary information is provided which needs to be assessed. The reader can learn what proportion of female managers had, for instance, less than five years' service. In other words, the pie charts provide a supplement to the text from which the reader can draw information. In some cases such information may enable the reader to come to a different conclusion from the writer, to criticize the assumptions made in the text, or to develop a new interpretation of the data.

(3) *Analytical*. The writer uses some statistical details in the text but is primarily concerned to establish general or theoretical observations based upon data which are separately represented in a table or chart. For example, it may be argued in the text that an employee's length of service is less important than that employee's gender in determining occupational position. In support of this assertion a series of bar charts may be produced comparing the length of service of different groups – male managers, female managers, male clerks, female clerks, etc. Here the onus is very much upon the reader to explore the data provided in order to evaluate its relevance to the writer's argument. The text may only touch on certain details whereas the reader must look closely at all the information in the charts and decide whether or not it does demonstrate the point made in the text.

These categories obviously overlap in practice, but they are provided to help illustrate the different functions which visual representation can play. For each of these categories the reader needs to follow some basic procedures, but as the proportion of new information incorporated in the diagram or chart increases so the job of interpretation becomes more important and more demanding. Every example of visual representation of statistical

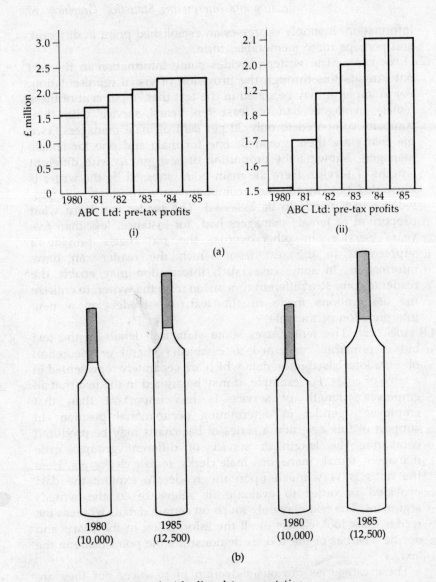

Figure 4.7 *Examples of misleading data presentation.*
(a) Two bar charts show that the pre-tax profits of the ABC company rose from just over 1.5 million pounds in 1980 to almost 2.1 million in 1984 and remained at that level in 1985. Note how the simple change of the scale on the y axis dramatically changes the chart's apparent message. Always check the calibration of such scales, especially to see if they begin from zero, and also whether the time scale is consistent and does not have misleading changes in the interval sizes.

data must be subjected to certain questions: is the chart clearly titled and labelled? Are the number, source and nature of the data clearly shown? Is it clear whether any figures are raw numbers or percentages? Are scales drawn accurately and are all the diagrams drawn to the same scale? To put it cynically, has the chart been 'doctored' in any way to make the data look more attractive, convincing or important than they really are? Figure 4.7 shows some examples of misleading data presentation and explains their effect.

When dealing with the Explanatory or Analytical categories especially, other questions also have to be asked. How were the data produced? In particular, are the categories and definitions used the most appropriate and might a change of category seriously alter the interpretation of the data? Are the data selected the most suitable to the argument being put forward? Should the data have been processed or analysed differently? Has the information been arranged in such a way as to minimize or maximize a particular pattern in the data? In short, visual representation has to be 'read' as carefully as any conventional text, so that its logic, its meaning and its completeness can be thoroughly assessed.

Summary

Social scientists encounter the world as a multiplicity of individual units but analyse it as a network of social groups. To accomplish this transformation they require conceptual and statistical procedures. The majority of the information produced by empirical research takes the form of single values associated with one case for a number of characteristics or variables: the number of years (= value) one employee (= case) has been working for a company (= variable). The researcher organizes these cases into aggregate first by constructing frequency distributions (both relative and cumula-

---

(b) Two pictograms showing that sales of Biffem cricket bats increased by 25 per cent between 1980 and 1985. In the first example only the height increases by 25 per cent, whereas in the second example all the dimensions grow, producing a bat which is much more impressive. Unfortunately it is also misleading, for the *area* of the second bat is not 25 per cent but 50 per cent bigger. This is a common trick utilized to dramatize increases in figures.

tive), and later by summarizing the pattern of these distributions in terms of proportions, percentages and ratios. In the process of doing this, important decisions have to be made regarding the categories into which data are placed, and the level at which the material is to be analysed. Inevitably some detail is lost, and some may be obscured, but the management of the data is achieved and it is this which is the prime statistical function at this stage.

Frequency distributions can be translated from numerical to diagrammatic form through the use of histograms, bar charts, pictograms and pie charts. These can be as simple or as elaborate as the resources and imagination of the researcher permits, but they must, ultimately, *increase* the accessibility of the information to other readers without sacrificing or compromising the accuracy of the original data. Consequently, the construction and presentation needs to be undertaken with care. The availability of 'graphics' on computers eases the manual effort involved in producing such charts but should not reduce the responsibility of the researcher to label, scale and arrange visual representation conscientiously.

Further exercises

A Using the variable 'Agegp' ('age' grouped), produce:
 (i) a relative and cumulative frequency distribution
 (ii) a block histogram
 (iii) a pie chart

Notes

1 L. Ott, R.F. Larson, and W. Mendenhall, *Statistics: A Tool for the Social Sciences* (3rd edn, Boston, Mass., Duxbury, 1983).

5 Summarizing the Data: Measures of Central Tendency and Dispersion

In the last chapter we concentrated on the process by which raw data are transformed into an ordered distribution. That distribution could then be described in terms of the number, proportion, or percentage of cases in any particular category, or the ratio of cases taking one value to those taking (one or more) other values. The whole distribution could be portrayed as a chart or diagram. In this chapter we look at statistics that are used to summarize an entire distribution in just a few figures: they do this by representing characteristics of the *shape* or *pattern* of the distribution. The best known of these are very common indeed – averages – but others may be unfamiliar: all can be understood in terms of the concept of dispersion.

5.1 Dispersion

Social scientists are forever looking for patterns, for regularities in data which reveal something of the social world. This is hardly surprising: the social world, by definition, consists of more or less regular and predictable patterns of action and behaviour. Sociological data which appeared to be entirely random would be as surprising as they would be confusing. The statistics of dispersion are the researcher's attempt to make simple statements about such patterns in any body of data.

In the analysis of any single variable distribution the researcher is faced with a *spread* of cases across a *range* of occurring values. There may be an obvious pattern to this spread of cases, or the researcher may produce a pattern through the selection of a smaller number of categories to represent the original, larger, number of values. This pattern will be of considerable interest. Beyond the initial task of counting cases (how many cases occur for each value), the next point of interest will be the shape of the distribution: are the cases spread evenly across the range of values? Are cases *clustered* together around a few similar values? Which category contains the highest number of cases, which the least? These are all questions about the *dispersion* of the cases: how cases are dispersed or spread across the range of occurring values. A glance at a histogram of a frequency distribution will illustrate this: figure 4.2 on page 60, for example. The histogram shows the rise and fall of the distribution; the high points and the low; the pattern in which the data are dispersed. Most importantly, it suggests to the researcher areas worth investigating further, and patterns that require explanation.

There are a number of ways of expressing the dispersion or pattern of a distribution statistically and these are normally divided into:

(a) measures of central tendency
(b) measures of dispersion
(c) distribution curves

The first is the simplest and the most familiar.

5.2 Measures of central tendency

In everyday speech these are what we would call 'averages', and consist of three separate measures: the *arithmetic mean*, the *median*, and the *mode*. The title 'measures of central tendency' derives from the fact that all our averages in some way represent the middle or central value in a frequency distribution. Each average, however, measures something slightly different and any difference between them reflects the characteristics of the particular distribution being studied.

The simplest of these three measures is the *mode*. This is just *the value which occurs most frequently*. Let's look again at the data used in chapter 4. Taking the raw data, the most frequently occurring value is 5; using the grouped data (table 4.2) the most popular category is '4 up to 6 years'. The mode has three advantages:

(a) it is very easy to identify
(b) it can be used with variables at any level of measurement

(c) it is useful when one is looking for the 'typical', the most common, value in a distribution

It has two disadvantages:

(a) it is a crude measure which does not take into consideration all the cases in a distribution
(b) it can be misleading when, in an otherwise fairly evenly spread distribution, the modal value happens to occur at one end of the range (i.e. a very high or very low value)

The *median* is *the value of the middle case* in a distribution arranged *cumulatively*. We have 357 cases. The middle of this series lies at case number 178. In the ungrouped distribution this case takes the value 5 so the median value is 5. In the grouped distribution this case falls in the category '4 and up to 6 years', so this is the median. The median can always be found by arranging a distribution cumulatively and locating the middle case. Remember that the 178th case in a cumulatively arranged distribution is not the same as case number 178 in the sample. Giving numbers to each case in the sample is simply for convenience and does not imply an order in frequency terms. If there is an odd number of cases in the sample then there will be a single middle case; if the sample has an even number of cases then we assume a hypothetical point between the two central cases. If, by some chance, the two central cases in a distribution take different values (say, for example, that one case had the value 5 and another the value 6), the procedure is simply to assume a middle value between the two (in this case 5.5). It is perhaps easiest to imagine the median as representing a line drawn through the middle of the distribution. On each side of the line there lies exactly 50 per cent of the cases: the median is the value at the middle of the distribution.

The median has two advantages:

(a) it is easy to identify from a cumulative distribution
(b) it represents the true middle of the data and is unaffected by the existence of values of the extremes of the range

It has two, slight, disadvantages:

(a) it can be used with ordinal and interval level variables but *not* with nominal level variables, as the values cannot be arranged in any hierarchical order

(b) it is based on only one case out of the whole distribution

The *arithmetic mean* is the measure which most people think of when they use the word average. The mean is calculated by adding together the values of all the cases in a distribution, and then *dividing the sum* (i.e. the total) *of the values by the number of cases*. This is expressed algebraically like this:

$$\bar{X} \text{ (the mean)} = \frac{\Sigma \text{ (the sum of all the values)}}{N \text{ (the number of cases)}}$$

(A glossary of simple algebraic terms can be found in Appendix B.)

The basic way of calculating the mean value for any distribution is to add all of the values from the raw data. This, however, will prove laborious if, as in our example, there are a large number of cases. In this instance we can work from the initial frequency distribution (see table 4.1). Each value that occurs is multiplied by the frequency with which it occurs, so, for our example:

Value (service in years)		*f* (frequency)
0	x	42
1	x	44
2	x	16
3	x	15
. . . .		

until a third column is produced, consisting of the values multiplied by their frequency.

Value ( )		*f*		*f*
0	x	42	=	0
1	x	44	=	44
. . . .				

The values in the third column are then added up, and the total divided by the number of cases (357). If we carry out this procedure for our sample we produce the following equation:

$$\frac{2491 \text{ (sum of values)}}{357 \text{ (no. of cases)}} = 6.9 \text{ (arithmetic mean)}$$

The mean has a number of advantages:

(a) it is simple to calculate and easily understood
(b) it takes into account all of the available values and cases
   But it has some disadvantages too:

(a) It must be used with interval level data, and cannot be used with nominal or ordinal level variables (although there is, as we shall see, a procedure for averaging grouped data)
(b) the inclusion of one or more values at the extremes of a distribution can distort the mean

This latter is the most important weakness of the mean and explains the difference in our three measures of central tendency.

As the three measures of central tendency essentially measure different characteristics of a distribution it is good practice always to calculate all three, where this is appropriate. The level of measurement determines which can be used and this will normally be evident to common sense (it is not possible to calculate the arithmetic mean of gender, or place of birth). The relationship between mean, median and mode, where all three can be calculated, also helps us to interpret the dispersion of cases. In a distribution where most of the cases are grouped close together, around a small range of values, then mean, median and mode will probably be quite similar. When cases are unevenly spread across a range of values or where there are a substantial number of cases at the top or bottom of a range, then the three measures might be fairly different. The 'averages', therefore, provide, individually, a single figure to represent the central or typical value in a distribution, and, analysed together, provide information about the pattern or dispersion of cases in a distribution.

In the situation where data are grouped and it is impossible to calculate an arithmetic mean from the raw data, then an estimation of the mean can be made by selecting the midpoint of each category to represent the whole category. This is then treated in exactly the same way as individual values in the calculation of an ungrouped mean: each midpoint is multiplied by the number of cases in that category; the resulting values are added together and divided by the total number of cases. Although calculating the mean in this way can be useful, and sometimes necessary, it must be remembered that at best it produces only a working estimate of the mean and should, consequently, be treated with some caution.

5.3 Measures of dispersion

Just as the measures of central tendency enable us to summarize the middle or average value in a distribution so those statistics labelled measures of dispersion enable us to summarize the spread of cases in a single figure. We have already used one of these extensively, and that is the simple concept of *range*. The range of a distribution is *the difference between the highest and lowest occurring values*. This can be expressed either by stating the two extremes of the range or, where appropriate, by calculating the difference between the two. The former can be used with ordinal or interval data, the latter with interval level data only. For example, for our variable *age* the range of values is from sixteen years to sixty-four years, a range of 48. But when the data are grouped (and therefore ordinal level) we can still state that the range is from sixteen years to sixty-four years. Range cannot be used with nominal variables because there exists no hierarchy and, consequently, no lowest or highest values.

The only measure of dispersion which can properly be used with nominal level variables is the simple percentage. Using percentages we can make descriptive statements about the spread of cases across the occurring values; the most and least popular category, the percentage of each cases in each category, and so on. Similarly, ordinal variables can only be described in fairly simple terms, but they do afford a little more scope. We can indicate the *range* of values in an ordinal variable (though not calculate a single figure for this) and we can use the statistical concept of *percentiles*. As the name suggests, these are similar to percentages, but are in fact an extension of the concept of the median. That measure, as we noted above, could best be regarded as a value at the numerical centre of a distribution, above and below which exactly 50 per cent of the cases lay. Percentiles simply apply this idea to a greater number of divisions: hypothetical lines are drawn through the data, not just at the midpoint (median) but at other places as well. Above and below each line a specific percentage of the cases in the distribution lie. Three examples of this technique should be noted:

(a) *Quartiles.* The distribution is divided into four equal parts. Twenty-five per cent of the cases fall in the first quartile, 50 per cent in the first two, etc.

(b) *Decile.* The distribution is divided into ten equal parts.

(c) *Percentile.* The distribution is divided into 100 equal parts. (This can only properly be used when there are more than 100 cases in the distribution.)

The median, therefore, can also be regarded as lying between the second and the third quartiles, or the fifth and sixth deciles. These measures are particularly useful when a researcher wants to state not just what percentage of cases took a particular value, but also what percentage of cases fall above or below a particular value or, indeed, what values the top 10, 20 or 50 per cent of the cases took.

It is, however, with interval level variables that we use the most important common measure of dispersion, which is called the *standard deviation* (represented algebraically as s or σ for the standard deviation of a sample or a population respectively). It is based on the measurement of the deviation or *difference of values from the mean value*. It tells us how much the values in a distribution differ from the average value which, in turn, gives an idea of how spread or dispersed the cases are across the whole range of values. Another way of looking at this would be to say that the standard deviation shows us how representative is the mean of the total distribution: in analysing dispersion the two figures, mean and standard deviation, are invariably used together.

The magnitude of the standard deviation is determined by two factors, the dispersion of the cases, and the size of the mean. It is important to remember both of these, as a large standard deviation figure does not necessarily mean a large amount of difference from the mean. It might just reflect the magnitude of the mean itself: in short, the two measures cannot safely be separated. The lowest value that the standard deviation can take is zero. Such a value would indicate that the values taken by cases in a distribution do not vary at all from the mean value: in other words, every case takes exactly the same value. This is, of course, highly unlikely but it helps us to interpret the standard deviation: the further from zero the measure is, relative to the mean, the greater the dispersion of cases from the mean. To look at it in terms of the mean: the smaller the standard deviation, relative to the mean, the more clustered the cases around the central value, and the more representative the mean is of the distribution as a whole.

The calculation of the standard deviation is a somewhat laborious process and it is highly unlikely that, in the age of calculators and computers, any social scientist is going to be engaged in performing this calculation manually. I shall, however, summarize the procedure in order to demonstrate more precisely what the standard deviation is actually measuring. The calculation can be done in five steps.

(a) Calculate the difference between each occurring value and the mean value; where a value occurs more than once, multiply the *difference* by the frequency with which the value occurs
(b) square each of these differences (that is, multiply it by itself)
(c) add together these squared differences
(d) divide the total by the number of cases
(e) take the square root of the resulting figure

Notice that we only square in order to get rid of negative values, and that this process is later reversed. Basically, the standard deviation is another mean: the sum of the differences divided by the number of cases. It is a sort of average difference from the mean.

If the calculation of this measure is unattractive, its use is not. Not only does it summarize dispersion in a single figure but together with the measures of central tendency it provides a concise description of a distribution's shape and pattern. The combination of these statistical measures with visual representation is probably the most valuable descriptive device available to the social scientist. The standard deviation is also useful in the comparison of different samples either with similar or different means. It permits the researcher to compare the dispersion of one sample with another or to compare the dispersion of cases in the same sample for two different variables. To illustrate its usefulness let's take both of the variables studied so far – length of 'service' and 'age'.

Calculating the standard deviation for the first variable (service) we find that it is 7.577; for the latter variable (age) the same measure is 13.929. How do we compare the dispersion of the two variables' distributions from these figures? First the other measures of dispersion need to be considered. The *range* of the variable 'service' is 39, smaller than the range of 48 for 'age', but this is partly a function of the different quantities involved: 'service' goes from 0 to 39, whereas 'age' begins at 16 extending to 64. This difference of quantity also effects the mean values: 6.9 for 'service', but 36.8 for 'age'. If we compare the other measures of central tendency we find that in both cases the values of the median and the mode are lower than the value of the mean (see table 5.1 for a computer printout of all these statistics). This suggests that for both variables there are a small number of cases taking high values which 'drag' the mean above the 'middle' cases. When we directly compare mean and deviation for each variable it is clear that *relative to the mean* the standard deviation for 'service' is much larger than that for 'age'. We can express this in a statistic called the *coefficient of variation*. This is simply produced by dividing the standard deviation by the mean, thus producing a standardized figure by which we can compare otherwise dissimilar distributions.

$$\text{Coefficient of Variation} = \frac{\text{standard deviation}}{\text{mean}}$$

The smaller the deviation in relation to the mean then the smaller will be the value of the coefficient of variation. For this example the figure for 'service' will be

$$\frac{7.577}{6.975} = 1.086$$

and for 'age' will be

$$\frac{13.929}{36.871} = 0.377$$

This confirms our impression of the measures and permits us a further interpretation of the statistics: the distribution of 'service' is more dispersed than that of 'age'. Or, to put it another way, the values in the distribution 'age' are less dispersed from the mean. The distributions are of a different shape and the pattern of dispersion for each is therefore also different. Such differences can be represented not just in statistics but in the diagrammatic form known as *distribution curves*.

Table 5.1 *Descriptive statistics for two variables (SPSS computer printout)*

(a) Service					
Mean	6.975	Median	4.816	Mode	5.000
STD DEV	7.577	Range	39.000		
Valid cases	357	Missing cases	0		
(b) Age					
Mean	36.871	Median	34.750	Mode	22.000
STD DEV	13.929	Range	48.000		
Valid cases	357	Missing cases	0		

5.4 Distribution curves

It should be clear from both this and the previous chapter that the social researcher is particularly interested in the shape of a frequency distribution, the extent to which it varies, the extent to which the location of cases is predictable or regular. In chapter 4 we noted the use of histogram, bar chart and the line called a polygon to represent and indicate pictorially the pattern of a distribution (see figures 4.1-4.4). This principle has been developed by statisticians in the use of *distribution curves*, continuous lines drawn to represent particular kinds of distribution. A distribution curve can be regarded as a model of a pattern of dispersion and, together with the procedures already covered, completes our statistical picture of dispersion.

By far the most important of all distribution curves is the *normal curve*. It is important because it portrays a type of distribution commonly found in social research, but also because, as a statistical model, it has properties which make it valuable to many other statistical procedures. I shall concentrate here on its place in descriptive statistics, rather than its more complex uses, and on its relation to the mean and standard deviation.

In the section above we noted (a) that a distribution in which the standard deviation was small relative to the mean would have a large proportion of cases clustered around that central value; and (b) that a distribution in which the mode, median and mean were all similar would have a regular pattern of dispersion with, again, a majority of cases close to the measures of central tendency. The *normal distribution* fits both of these descriptions. Indeed, it should be seen as the model of such distributions for it is not a real-life distribution but an ideal type displaying these characteristics. The normal distribution has mean, median and mode identical; inevitably it is symmetrical and regular, for 50 per cent of the cases lie on each side of the central value; the dispersion of cases in the distribution can be described through a calculation of the mean and standard deviation. Figure 5.1 shows a normal curve drawn as a hypothetical distribution: it is bell-shaped, symmetrical about its mean, and contains all the cases in the distribution in the area under the curve.

All normal curves are the same shape but they may vary in their *peakedness*. That is, some curves may be flatter than others, some more steep or peaked (see figure 5.2). The smaller the standard

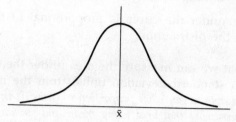

Figure 5.1 *The normal curve, representing a distribution which is symmetrical about its mean.*

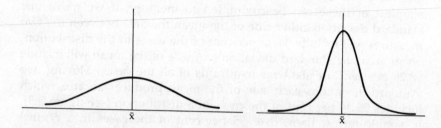

Figure 5.2 *Two more normal curves, distinguished by their peakedness*

deviation, the more peaked the curve; the larger the standard deviation the flatter the curve. Peakedness, in other words, is just a way of measuring the clustering or dispersion of cases from the mean in a normal distribution. It also has some use as a descriptive concept with distribution curves in general.

In real-life distributions we may not find the normal curve in its ideal form but we do find this kind of pattern frequently enough to make it a valuable model, and to allow us to utilize the special properties of the normal curve. It is important to bear in mind, though, that the normal curve is a *type* of curve rather than any particular distribution produced in research. It might help to treat it in the same way as we treat a sociological concept such as status or alienation – not as an exact description of reality but as an aid to understanding reality by providing an ideal definition from which to work.

To understand the unique mathematical properties of the normal curve it is necessary to remember that because of its shape,

(a) it can be defined statistically in terms of its mean and its standard deviation;

(b) the area under the curve is proportional to the number of cases in the distribution.

This means that we can measure the area under the curve in terms of distance (in standard deviation units) from the mean. In other words, *it is possible to say what proportion of cases lie in any area under the curve by measuring that area using mean and standard deviation*. In fact, the symmetry of the normal curve means that, regardless of the actual mean and standard deviation, there will always be a constant area between the mean and any given point on the axis. The simplest of these can be committed to memory: if we move one standard deviation either side of the mean the area between the two measures will include 34.13 per cent of the cases in the distribution. So an area one standard deviation *each* side of the mean will include 68.26 per cent, or just over two-thirds of all the cases. Moving two standard deviations each side of the mean produces an area which includes 95.46 per cent of the cases in a distribution (see figure 5.3). In simple terms, then, over 95 per cent of the cases in a normal distribution will lie in an area two standard deviations each side of the mean. This gives a clear illustration of exactly what the standard deviation measures, and demonstrates that, in a normal distribution, the dispersion of cases has a regularity and a predictability definable in terms of mean and standard deviation.

Having established the principle of measuring the area under the normal curve it is possible to apply it to any area at all using the standard deviation as a unit and measuring in units, and fractions of units, from the mean. This ability to predict the dispersion of cases in a normal distribution is the basis of other statistical procedures, both in *sampling* (where we are concerned with the representativeness of a sample taken from a larger population), and in testing *hypotheses* (where we are interested in the elimination of chance or error). The social scientist also encounters many distributions in research which approximate the normal curve and thus can be understood in terms of its particular characteristics.

It might be objected at this point that many distributions found in social research could not be described in the terms of the normal distribution. This is true and two other statistical concepts are useful to describe other types of distribution curve, though neither of these enjoys the special properties or importance of the normal curve. A *skewed* curve is one in which the mean, median and mode do not coincide and in which cases lie disproportionately at one end of the range of values. A distribution in which the mean is 'pulled'

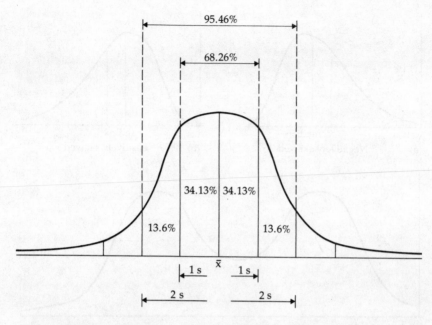

Figure 5.3 *The normal distribution curve showing the percentage of cases included in areas one and two standard deviations from the mean*

towards one extreme of the range by the inclusion of a few very high or very low values will be represented as a skewed curve. Figure 5.4 shows two skewed curves. The direction of *skewness* depends on the position of the mean and median: a distribution in which the mean is less than (to the left of) the median is *negatively skewed*; where the mean is greater than (to the right of) the median, the curve is *positively skewed*. The extent of skewness can be measured, but seldom is, as social science has more use for the descriptive than the mathematical power of such concepts. The distributions for both 'service' and 'age', discussed above are positively skewed.

Finally, we should mention the *bimodal* distribution. The normal curve and the skewed curves illustrated are all unimodal, that is, they have one mode, one highest point. However it is not uncommon to find distributions which have two modes or at least two peaks in the dispersion of cases. Figure 5.4(c) shows a model bimodal curve but it is more usual to encounter a distribution in which there is one real mode, but a second, slightly lesser, peak in the distribution.

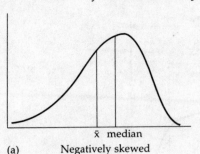

x̄ median

(a)   Negatively skewed

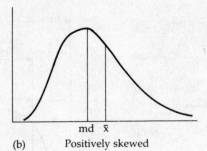

md x̄

(b)   Positively skewed

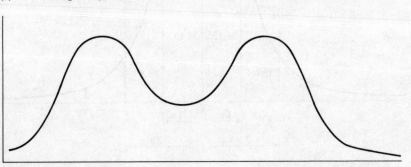

(c)

Figure 5.4(a) and (b) *Skewed distribution curves (note that the mean is less than the median in a negatively skewed curve, but greater than the median in a positively skewed curve); (c) Bimodal curve: the two peaks do not need to be identical and are unlikely to be in real-life distributions.*

Summary

The distribution of cases in a sample will be different for each variable which we study; the distribution of cases across the same variable will be different for two different samples. Social scientists need a way of summarizing the spread and pattern of cases so that such comparisons can be made easily and with statistical accuracy: measures of central tendency, measures of dispersion, and distribution curves provide that way. The most powerful of these (mean, standard deviation, normal distribution) can only be used with interval level data but the other measures which can be used with ordinal variables, or which are universally applicable, are not to be disparaged: any description of dispersion allows us a greater understanding of the data and thus helps to explain its particular character.

Further exercises

A Repeat the calculation of the measures shown in table 5.1 using only the *sample cases* (n=89). What can you say about each distribution from its measures of central tendency and dispersion? How do the figures compare with the figures for the whole population of cases (n=357)?

6 Taking a Sample: Inductive Statistics

Before any researcher can confront a set of data with statistical techniques those data must be produced, and it is again statistical procedures which enable us to do this. I mentioned in chapter 3 the distinction between a *population* (all of the cases in which the researcher is interested) and a *sample* (a proportion of cases drawn from that population). Very often in the social sciences we are concerned with taking a sample in order to draw conclusions about the population from which it was taken. That is, we use the sample as a basis for generalizing about the population. This process constitutes the subject matter of *inductive* or *inferential* statistics: we infer or induce the characteristics of the population from the characteristics of the sample.

6.1 Why use a sample?

The primary reason for using samples is practicality. We are often studying a population which would be too large to be dealt with in a single study. There are always limits on time and expenditure; research is, unavoidably, guided by issues of practical constraint; commonly, the sample is the social scientist's only means of evaluating the characteristics of a much larger social group. Faced with finite resources and the choice between studying a large population superficially or a sample from that population in some detail, the researcher will often find the latter a more attractive choice. When the population of interest is small or when the relevant data are already recorded (for example in government official statistics), a sample may not be necessary – although in the latter instance, the social scientist may still want to construct a case study based on a new sample in order to make comparisons with official data.

Indeed, we might consider the typical sociological case study as a kind of sample, even when it includes the whole of a specified population, because such studies are frequently used to illustrate or represent much more general social groups. For example, the data in chapters 4 and 5 were taken from a study of office workers and consisted of data on all of the workers in a particular organization – the population under study. However, in one sense the cases might be regarded as a quasi-sample in as much as the information from that study could be used by the researchers to illustrate the position of office workers in general. This is no more than re-stating the point that in social research we are interested in making general statements about collectivities and that we use our study of small parts of the social world to illuminate the social world as a whole. This relationship is illustrated below:

The position of clerical workers	←	General problem/ Social world
Clerical workers in Organization A	←	Selected issue/ Case study
All clerical workers in Company A	←	Population
Percentage of clerical workers in Company A	←	Sample

Clearly, the social researcher has a considerable responsibility to ensure that, at every stage of the research process, the data being produced are as representative as possible of the social group or population from which they have been drawn. Sampling procedures and inductive statistics help in this but ultimately they are not a substitute for clarity of thought: the researcher must have a clear idea of the purpose of the research and the justification for a particular population and/or sample being chosen.

6.2 Why do samples work?

The theory of sampling rests on the assumption that there is conformity in the behaviour of individuals and, consequently, in the distribution of cases in any population. As we saw in our study of dispersion (chapter 5) this is true in many instances. Although cases may be dispersed across the whole range of values, it is rare to find an even pattern of dispersion: cases tend to be grouped together, particularly around the central values, expressed by the mean, median and mode. This is particularly true of the normal distribution which typifies the dispersion pattern often found in social research. It is also true that the larger the population the more likely a distribution is to assume the pattern of the normal curve. This is because the extreme values have a diminishing influence on the distribution and the pattern of the distribution becomes increasingly predictable with increasing size.

The normal distribution is important to sampling techniques because it demonstrates this conformity of distribution; it also enables us to make statistical estimations of the distribution of cases using the mean and standard deviation. It demonstrates that for any particular variable only a certain number of possible values exist and that these values occur in a fairly regular pattern. Given a large enough number of cases that pattern is statistically predictable. Working from this knowledge we can understand that each sample, in theory, is the population in miniature. *The characteristics of the sample approximate the characteristics of the population* because the distribution of cases in the population is regular and predictable and the distribution of cases in the sample will be predictable in the same way.

The characteristics of a population are referred to as *parameters*; the characteristics of a sample are called *statistics*. This may seem a little confusing but they are basically the same measurements for different sets of cases: the mean value of a variable in a sample is a statistic; the mean value of the same variable in the population is a parameter. Normally, the researcher will not be in a position to know what the parameter is, but will be able to calculate the statistic: it is from the sample statistics that we can infer the population parameters. The two values need not be the same, indeed they are unlikely to be so, but they will be fairly similar and we can estimate how similar they are likely to be without knowing the population parameter. The larger the sample we take, the smaller the difference between statistic and parameter. Equally if a number of samples are taken from the same population and then, although the statistics of each sample may be different, combined together the statistics of the sample will more closely approximate the population parameters. Whereas, normally, a parameter is *fixed* but *unknown*, a statistic is *known* but may *vary* from one sample to another.

In practice, of course, the very constraints that force the researcher to take a sample ensure that only one, perhaps fairly small, sample can be taken. The statistical basis of sampling (in particular the predictability of the normal distribution), however, ensures that the sample can be representative and that the researcher can estimate how representative it is. This difference between a parameter and a statistic is called the *sampling error* and is made up of two elements:

(a) *Random sampling error.* This is always present and reflects the fact that the sample can never be identical to the population. The larger the sample the smaller the random sampling error.
(b) *Bias.* This is error due to mistakes or inaccuracies during the sampling procedure. It may not always be possible to eliminate bias but careful sampling can minimize its effect.

To summarize, then, the use of sampling permits the social scientist to make observations about populations which it would be impractical to study in full. Our knowledge of the statistical properties of distribution curves provides the information necessary to evaluate the representativeness of a sample and to estimate population parameters from sample statistics.

6.3 Sampling procedures

The process of constructing a sample consists, like other research procedures, as much of definition as it does of data collection: indeed the latter cannot take place satisfactorily without the former having been carefully undertaken. The first step is, obviously enough, to define what it is you are sampling. A sample does not have to consist of people – each case may be one firm, the incidence of a crime, a household unit. Normally this definition is a matter of common sense but it is not always self-evident. Take the example of a sociologist interested in studying the characteristics of immigrant families in an English town: is the basic unit of study the household (i.e. the whole family), the adults in the household, or each family member individually? Such a decision makes the researcher think more carefully about the aim of the research and the information that might be produced by selecting any particular sample.

The most commonly known samples are those taken by private companies either in opinion polling or in market research. Social research and government surveys also use samples, and most members of the public are familiar with the questionnaire, sent through the post or administered by an interviewer, so commonly used in survey samples. A survey does not, of course, have to be a sample. The largest survey carried out in this country, the decennial census, has (in theory at least) the literal population as its population of study. The sample survey, then, is a particular sort of survey in which a selection of cases are taken to represent a much larger, but inaccessible, population of cases.

Having defined our area of interest, the next step is to define the population from which the sample will be drawn. Again we are faced with problems of definition. Take the example of the data used in the preceding chapters – office workers in an administrative organization. A researcher wishing to take a sample of workers from this organization first decides that the population consists of 'all office workers employed by the organization'. However, this is still only a very general definition and needs to be turned into an *operational definition* (see chapter 2, section 2.2.4) – one which can be used in the actual process of measurement and quantification. It will be necessary to define 'office worker' more carefully; which employees should be included in this category? Should the researcher adopt the categories used by the organization itself or generate a working definition for the survey? Just as fundamentally, how is the 'organization' defined? Does it include employees working outside the main offices, in local branches for example, or clerical workers located at warehouses or factories? Finally, what are we to mean by 'employed'? Will it include part-time workers, casual workers, workers who are on training schemes or work experience courses? In short, the construction of an operational definition requires the researcher to consider the meaning of every category and concept, however self-evident it may initially appear. To the newcomer to quantitative research this may seem remarkably fastidious, nitpicking even, but the researcher must be absolutely certain what the data are going to represent: once the characteristics, attitudes and opinions of those in the sample are transformed into codes, numbers and statistical figures there is no leeway for changing definitions, for modifying the procedures, or for correcting discrepancies; the preparation must be as good as possible from the outset.

Once the population is defined we need a list of all the cases in the population from which a sample can be drawn. This is called a *sampling frame*. In this example the sampling frame would be the organization's personnel files, listing all the employees. In market research or opinion polling where households are being contacted the local Register of Electors is a common sampling frame, as is a local telephone directory, or a directory of local streets and households. A sociologist investigating the incidence of a certain crime may use court records as a sampling frame; an economist studying large corporations might use an index of the 'top 1,000 firms' to establish the population. Whatever is used it must be remembered that the sampling frame may not be precisely identical to the operational definition of the population.

In our example, for instance, personnel records may not be fully up-to-date – very recent employees may not be documented; recent changes in job, grade, salary or location may not have been recorded; the grading structure, pay structure, or even departmental titles may have been altered. Any such anomalies or omissions should be noted by the researcher since they are potential sources of *bias* in the sample and need to be accounted for.

The sample should be drawn, therefore, from the best possible sampling frame representing a clearly defined population: the next decisions can then be about the sample itself. The most obvious question will be how big the sample should be, and this will be determined by two factors: the resources available for the research and the degree of precision required. The first factor will determine issues such as the duration of the research and the number of people who could be interviewed; the latter is important because the larger the sample, relative to the population, the closer the sample statistics to the population parameters. Normally, the researcher will aim to achieve the largest sample compatible with the resources available, but it may be that a smaller sample is desirable if the study is to concentrate on complex characteristics which would require, for example, in-depth interviewing.

Once we have decided what proportion of the cases to include in the sample these cases must be selected and this is done by taking a *random sample* of cases from the population. A random sample has been well defined by Reichmann as:

> a sample which is drawn from a population in such a way that every member of the population has an equal chance of selection as a member of the sample, and that inclusion or exclusion from the sample could not be affected by any factor other than chance.[1]

Such a procedure minimizes the possibility of bias entering the sample and permits the researcher to treat the sample as a statistically reliable representation of the population. The actual procedure for taking a random sample is straightforward enough. Statisticians have constructed something called a 'table of random numbers' which is quite simply a series of numbers occurring randomly, that is without any fixed or arranged pattern. (A table of random numbers can be found in Appendix 5.) The researcher then numbers each of the cases in the population (remembering to begin 01 if there are up to 99 cases, or 001 if there are more than 99) and begins reading along any row of a random numbers table. Every time a number occurs in the table which also occurs in the list of cases then that case becomes part of the sample. The procedure continues until the required number of cases has been selected.

There are, of course, even simpler ways of taking a sample. If we have decided to include 10 per cent of the population in the sample then we might simply choose every tenth case from the sampling frame. However, this may not give a truly representative sample if the sampling frame itself is organized in a non-random way. A list of employees, for example, may be organized by department such that employees with certain characteristics may be grouped together and, on the 'every nth case' system, will not have an equal chance of being selected. Any departure from randomness weakens the statistical representativeness of the sample.

6.4 Non-random sampling

The social scientist is quite often in the position of constructing a sample on criteria other than purely random selection. The most common reason for this will be the researcher's desire to include within the sample a specific proportion of certain cases, or representative cases from sections of the population which might, in a random sample, not be selected. Alternatively, an adequate sampling frame may not be available or the population's precise size not known. In such instances other sampling procedures may be used either instead of or, more frequently, in conjunction with, random sampling. Three are worthy of notice.

(1) *Stratified sampling*. This is probably the most common situation for the social researcher. The population being studied is not homogeneous in certain respects and the researcher wants to allow

for this by sub-dividing the population prior to sampling. If, for instance, the researcher knows that only a very small proportion of a population of office employees are Asian immigrants but is interested in comparing their characteristics and attitudes to those of other employees, the 'immigrant' cases would have to be identified and separated out to ensure that some of their number were selected for the final sample. This is called a *stratified sample*. The original population is stratified, divided into sub-groups, and then a random sample can be taken from each group or stratum. This ensures that each sub-group of interest is sampled but that a degree of randomness is retained with respect to the actual individual cases selected. It also remains possible to combine the samples by a technique called *weighting*. In this procedure a *weight* or number is assigned to each stratum in inverse proportion to the stratum's probability of being selected from the population. By multiplying the value produced for each stratum by its respective weight the effect of their different chances of selection can be reduced and the statistics from each sample can be directly compared or combined. In this way the mean values of variables from each sample can be combined to produce a *weighted average* for the aggregated sample.[2]

(2) *Cluster or multi-stage sampling*. This is used where the population is divided into separate groups or constituencies, each of which can be treated as a sub-population. It is used when sampling is, for example, organized on a geographical basis and distinct areas within a population might initially be sampled individually. Again, samples can later be combined into a sample of the whole population by the use of weighting.

(3) *Quota sampling*. This is a technique used more in market than social research where some characteristics of the population may be known but the population itself cannot be comprehensively defined. Consequently, the researcher determines the characteristics required in the sample, and selects cases which fulfil these characteristics. For example, a market research company may be interested in the orientation of young married women to a new product. Interviewers are sent out with instructions to interview a fixed number of people, at least 75 per cent of whom must be married women under the age of 35. Clearly this betrays the rules of random selection, and risks introducing considerable error in the interviewer's selection of cases. It would only be used by the social scientist when a relatively approximate guide to a population was required: such a sample could not have a strong claim to representativeness.

6.5 Sampling in practice

Let us suppose that the 357 cases in our office population about which we have information constitutes too large a number for the purposes of further research. Initial data was produced, let us say, through a study of personnel records but the next stage of the research necessitates fairly lengthy interviews with individual employees. The researcher does not have sufficient time and assistance to carry out 357 interviews and consequently decides to take a sample which will constitute a smaller, interview group.

Estimating the time and resources available, the researcher decides that it would be feasible to interview about one-quarter of the population. Interviewing one worker in four would give a total sample of 89 cases which would fulfil the criteria both of being substantially smaller than the population yet also large enough to include a reasonable cross-section of the original population. The sampling frame already exists in the form of the original, numbered, lists of cases and the sample can be drawn from this using a random numbers table (see Appendix 5).

Starting at column 1, row 1, on the random numbers table (although it is in fact possible to start at *any* point in the table) we read from left to right, treating the figures as a series of three-digit numbers, thus – *104* 801 501 *101* 536 *020 118 164* 791 646 691 791 419. Of the first 13 numbers, 5 correspond to case numbers in the population and, consequently, become the first 5 cases in the sample. The procedure is simply continued until 89 cases have been selected in this manner. In Appendix 1 those cases selected for the sample using this method are marked with an asterisk.

This, however, is not necessarily the final form of the sample. A sample selected for interviewing, whether direct interviewing or by postal questionnaire, has to be contacted. It is at this stage of the sampling process that further error and bias can be introduced through alterations to the random sample. Basically, cases selected from the population may not appear in the final sample because of either non-contact or non-response.

1 *Non-contact.* In this situation the individual simply cannot be contacted after being selected for interview. They may have moved, left the company, be ill or otherwise unavailable; or the original sampling frame may have provided a mistaken name, address or other details.

2 *Non-response.* In this situation the individual is contacted

successfully but is unable or unwilling to participate in the research. Similarly they may agree to participate, reluctantly, but provide inadequate responses leading the interviewer to discount the information they have provided.

Non-contact is a particular problem when the sample being studied is geographically inaccessible, or transient, or can only be contacted at limited times. *Non-response* is a problem when postal questionnaires are being used or, in an administered interview, when there is organizational hostility or suspicion of the research.

If the level of non-contact or non-response becomes too high then it is likely that the sample is going to be biased in some respect. Specifically, the researcher is faced with the problem of *self-selection*. This describes the situation where, with a high level of non-response, those who do participate in the research can be seen as having distinct characteristics and attitudes: unlike some of their fellows they are predisposed to participate and may hold different opinions, along with their favourable, or at least non-hostile, view of social research. Conversely, the non-respondents may constitute a definite attitudinal group whose lack of interest in the research may go along with other characteristics. On comparing the two groups the researcher may find, for example, that on average, the non-respondents are older than those who participated; or that they come predominantly from one part of the organization. In short, *the larger the proportion of 'missing' cases, the more suspicious the researcher must be of the representativeness of the sample.*

Unfortunately, it is impossible to state categorically how large or small a sample should be; or at what level the phenomena of non-contact and non-response significantly bias the sample. As a guideline researchers often quote 70 per cent response as a 'good' response rate for a postal survey, and expect rather higher rates for interviewing carried out face to face. This, however, should be treated with some caution as each population and sample differ. Two factors should be taken into consideration besides the gross response rate: the size of the sample, and the information available about non-respondents. The first is important since a small sample, especially when it represents only a small proportion of the population, is more vulnerable to bias and the inclusion or exclusion of even a few cases can have a disproportionate effect on the final data. Low response rates should not be so worrying if the sample is large and constitutes a substantial proportion of the original population. The second factor is important because if the researcher has data available about the non-response then it becomes possible to assess whether the non-respondents have similar characteristics (age, gender, position etc.) which might cause their exclusion to bias the sample. Clearly this is only possible when some information is known about the population, or at least the planned sample, before interviewing. If the non-response itself appears to be random then the representativeness of the sample is not so much in doubt.

6.6 Comparing the sample and the population

In a great deal of social research the statistical data produced as part of the sample remain the prime or sole focus of analysis. The value of sample theory in such cases is twofold: it enables the researcher to generalize from the sample data with some confidence that the sampling is representative of a much broader population; and it provides a procedure for constructing a sample which is designed to minimize bias. It is less common for the researcher to want to produce estimates of the actual population parameters from the sample statistics produced but this is possible, statistically, and conventionally, statistics textbooks have devoted a relatively large amount of space to this. This will not be done here for two reasons. Firstly, I believe that for the practising social scientist it is the principle and mechanics of constructing a sample which are, overwhelmingly, of the greatest relevance; and, secondly, because a book of this size is explicitly designed as an introduction and does not aspire to cover detailed procedures which have been comprehensively catalogued in much larger volumes. Nevertheless, it is worthwhile mentioning in outline at least the procedures by which sample and population can be statistically compared.

6.7 Estimating the population mean from the sample mean

If we wish to infer a population parameter for a particular variable from its sample statistic we use a technique called *estimation*. Basically we want to know how much the sample statistic differs from the population parameter or, in other words, how accurate a representation the sample statistic is of the population parameter. To put this into practice we utilize three concepts:

(a) the normal distribution

(b) the standard error
(c) confidence levels

If we want to know how close the sample mean of a variable is to the population mean then we need to know how much this sample mean (and any other sample means we could produce) vary from the population mean. If we can assume that the population is *normally distributed* then we know that the difference of any values from the mean can be measured in terms of *standard deviation* units. Therefore we use the standard deviation of the sample mean(s) to estimate the variance of the sample mean from the population mean. In sampling theory this is called the *standard error* and is calculated by dividing the standard deviation of the population by the square root of the sample size. Here, however, we encounter a problem, since we do not know the standard deviation of the population and cannot calculate it. We do know, though, that the standard deviation of the sample is likely to be relatively close to the standard deviation of the population and, accordingly, we substitute the former for the latter in our equation. Therefore,

$$\sigma \bar{X} \text{ (Standard Error)} = \frac{S \text{ (standard deviation of the sample)}}{\sqrt{n} \text{ (square root of the sample size)}}$$

Once we have calculated the standard error then we can use it just like a standard deviation in a normal distribution. That is, we can assume that a fixed proportion of cases lie within one, two or three standard deviations of the mean and consequently we can predict the area within which the population mean will fall by calculating its distance from the sample mean in units of standard error. An example will help to illustrate this procedure.

Taking our sample data generated in section 6.5 above we can calculate the (mean) average *age* of the workers included in the sample. Table 6.1 shows a frequency distribution for the variable 'age' using the sample data only. The mean age can be calculated as 39.4 years, and the standard deviation is 14.2. Assuming that the distribution of the population as a whole for this variable at least approximates a normal distribution then we can calculate the standard error.

Using the formula above we produce the following:

Table 6.1 *Frequency distribution for the variable age (sample data)*

Age Value (x)	Relative frequency (fx)
16	1
17	1
18	1
19	4
20	3
21	4
22	6
23	2
25	1
26	1
28	1
29	1
30	1
32	6
34	1
35	5
36	1
37	1
38	2
40	2
41	4
43	1
44	1
45	3
46	1
48	3
49	1
50	6
51	1
53	3
54	2
55	4
56	2
57	2
58	1
59	3
60	4
61	2
62	1

No. of cases (n) = 89
Mean age (x̄) = 39.4   Standard Deviation(s) = 14.2

$$\text{σ}\bar{\text{X}} \text{ (standard error)} = \frac{14.2}{\sqrt{89}} \text{ , or}$$

$$\text{σ}\bar{\text{X}} = \frac{14.2}{9.44} \text{ , thus}$$

$$\text{σ}\bar{\text{x}} = 1.50$$

How then do we use this standard error figure? In chapter 5 we discussed the use of the standard deviation to measure the proportion of cases falling a given distance from the mean. We saw that a constant percentage of all cases in a normal distribution fell one (68 per cent), two (95 per cent) and three (99 per cent) standard deviations each side of the mean. We can apply precisely the same principle in this case, but using the standard error. Since, for example, 95 per cent of cases lie within two standard deviations of the mean, then, similarly, 95 per cent of all sample means must fall within two standard errors of the true population mean. We are therefore able to estimate the range of values within which the population mean will lie. Harper puts it concisely: 'This means that if we take a single sample, then 19 times out of 20 the sample mean will lie within two standard errors of the true mean of the population.'[3]

In this example, then, we can estimate that the population mean should fall within two standard errors (2 × 1.50) either side of the sample mean (39.4). That is, the population mean lies between 36.4 and 42.4.

Using two standard errors from the mean gives us a 95 per cent chance of correctly locating the range within which the population mean lies. We may decide, however, that a 5 per cent chance of being wrong is too great, in which case we can extend our range to three standard errors from the mean. This area will include over 99 per cent of cases, that is, virtually all of the variation from the mean. Recalculating our example using this larger range we find that the population mean falls between 34.9 and 43.9.

Whichever figure we choose (95 or 99 per cent) is called a *confidence level*. In other words it represents *the certainty or confidence with which we can predict the location of a population mean*. Estimations of this kind must always indicate what level of confidence is being used. Later on we will encounter the confidence level again in a slightly different guise, that of the *level of significance*. This measure is given as a decimal fraction (e.g. 0.001) but has fundamentally the same meaning. A significance level of 0.001 means a chance of one in one hundred that a statistic is unreliable – in other words 99 per cent confidence; a level of 0.005 means five chances in 100, or 95 per cent confidence. Both, very similar, concepts are widely used in the measurement of probability in statistical relationships.

6.8 The use of Student's 't' distribution

The estimation of a population mean using the standard error is fairly accurate while the size of the sample is large and normally distributed. It is also useful in conveying an idea of the statistical relation between a sample and the population from which it is drawn. However, because it relies on substituting the sample mean and standard deviation for that of the population, some inaccuracy is inevitable. This assumes much greater importance when the sample we are dealing with is small and may not be a normal distribution. Consequently, a more accurate means of estimation, appropriate for small samples, has been developed and this is called *Student's t-test*.

This test is based on the 't' distribution which is similar to, but flatter than, a normal distribution. It is calculated using the known sample statistics which we have already used: the mean, standard deviation, and the number of cases. However, the procedure for utilizing Student's 't' relies upon a number of concepts which we have not previously encountered. These may appear cumbersome at first but they are valuable and widely used statistical ideas. One of these is the *level* of *significance* which, as we mentioned in section 6.7 above, is another expression of the concept of *confidence level*. When using Student's t-test we must select a level of significance which will satisfy the requirements of our analysis. Most commonly this will be either 0.005 (95 per cent confidence) or 0.001 (99 per cent confidence). Level of significance is normally represented by the letter p. For example, the statement

$$p = 0.0006$$

indicates that a test statistic is significant at the level 0.0006 (i.e. there are only six chances in 1,000 that the statistic is unreliable). If, in this instance, the researcher has selected a level of significance of 0.001 as adequate, it may be enough to state that p › 0.001

meaning that the statistic is significant at a level *greater than* the selected level of 0.001.

Another important concept to understand is that of the *null hypothesis*. In quantitative sociology we are frequently dealing with *hypotheses*, that is statements about the character of variables, or the relationships between variables, that can be empirically tested. In many statistical procedures it is assumed that a hypothesis will be stated in a formal way so that it can be rejected. This is important as it enables us to state precisely what we are testing and, therefore, what evidence is required to reject, or refute the hypothesis. Such a formal statement is called the null hypothesis, as it takes the form of a hypothesis that we can reject by testing. In other words the null hypothesis is contradicted by the *research hypothesis*, the theory or assertion the researcher believes to be true. Although it is impossible to prove something to be unequivocally true, we can affirm or support a hypothetical assertion by rejecting a contradictory hypothesis. Thus if we test a null hypothesis and find there is enough evidence to reject it, then we have actually helped to verify our original research hypothesis.

As useful as it is to talk in terms of testing and refuting hypotheses, it is worth remembering that the research process is not always such a neat and tidy process. As we discussed in chapter 2.2, the model of research procedure can often be contradicted by the less tractable problem of real-life research. Although researchers may operate with one or more research hypotheses, these may remain in a very generalized form and could not be accurately tested. It is often only after considerable exploratory research that testable hypotheses can be confidently produced.

One more complication arises with the testing of hypotheses of this kind. We need to be clear whether we are interested in the *direction* of the difference between our null hypothesis and our research hypothesis. To put it as simply as possible, do we, for example, reject the null hypothesis in order to show that a population mean is *greater than* a sample mean, or do we reject it to show that it is *not the same as* the sample mean. Occasionally, we will merely be interested in demonstrating that a population parameter is not of a certain value, but, more frequently, our research hypothesis will include an assumption about the direction in which the population differs from the sample.

In statistical terms this distinction is embodied in the *one-tailed* or *two-tailed* test. If the researcher wants to know simply whether or not a population parameter differs significantly from an observed sample statistic, then a two-tailed test can be used. The 'tails' here refer to the tails, or extreme limits, of a distribution curve (see chapter 5). If, however, the researcher wishes to know specifically whether the parameter is greater than, or less than, the statistic a one-tailed test is used. We are simply finding out whether the parameter falls in the tail of a particular range of values. A glance at the t value table will show that, for any given level of significance, *the t value required for a two-tailed test to be significant is higher than that required for a one-tailed test.* Using the t distribution, a negative value of t indicates a value in the left-hand tail of the curve; a positive value, one in the right-hand side of the curve. So, to reject a null hypothesis on a one-tailed test the t value must be either greater than the t value specified in the table (suggesting that the parameter is significantly greater than the statistic); or if it is a negative value it must be less than a negative value of t in the table.

This will undoubtedly appear confusing at first encounter, but a relatively simple example illustrates the use of t; all the working for this example is reproduced in table 6.2. First we take a much smaller sample (N=20) from our population, and select a characteristic to measure: here we have taken the average length of service of employees. We can see that for our small sample the average (mean) service is equal to 4.75 years. Assume that we cannot know the population mean and that this is a small, randomly selected, sample drawn from a population the parameters of which we do not know. However, in other comparable populations the average length of service of employees has always been less than nine years, and our research hypothesis is that this population will also have a mean of less than nine years. The sample mean is clearly less than nine, but we have to use the t-test to establish whether that sample mean (from a very small sample) is a reliable guide.

Our first step therefore is to state our research hypothesis and to frame a null hypothesis, in a way that it can be rejected by testing. If our null hypothesis is that the population mean is equal to nine, then a rejection of this, using a one-tailed test, will allow us to accept with a reasonable level of confidence our research hypothesis.

Our next step is to calculate a value for our test statistic, t. If this value is significant at a chosen level of significance, then the null hypothesis can be rejected. The researcher may then wish to accept the research hypothesis.

Table 6.2   *Using the t-test on a small sample*

i Sample of 20 cases randomly selected from population:

Case no. 058   010   015   091   355   340   350   342   084   223
            337   039   032   209   263   320   176   173   001   272

ii Variable to be tested = service. Value of this variable for each case in the sample:

Service 5   5   1   1   18   8   1   18   5   1
          7   5   0   0   10   0   0   3   0   7

iii Average (mean) length of service of sample cases:
$\bar{X} = 4.75$ years

iv Standard deviation of sample values:
$s = 5.34$

v Null hypothesis: that the population mean for the variable 'service' is equal to nine years:
$\mu = 9.0$ years

vi Use the t-test formula to test this hypothesis, selecting the 0.005 level of significance.

$$t = \frac{\bar{X} - \mu}{s/\sqrt{N}-1} = \frac{4.75 - 9.0}{5.34/\sqrt{20}-1}$$

$$= \frac{-4.25}{5.34/4.36} = \frac{-4.25}{1.22} = -3.48$$

vii At 0.005 level of significance a value of 2.861 (or −2.861) would be required to reject the null hypothesis.

viii For our sample test, t = −3.48 therefore p› 0.005:
we can reject the null hypothesis.

ix Accept the research hypothesis that the population mean is less than nine years: μ‹ 9.0

The value of t can be calculated by subtracting the population mean from the sample mean and dividing the resulting figure by the sample deviation, divided by the square root of the number of cases minus one. Algebraically, this is

$$t = \frac{\bar{X} - \mu}{s/\sqrt{N}-1}$$

Clearly, here the population mean is what we are testing so it must be replaced in the equation by our *assumed* mean (the assumption embodied in the null hypothesis). So, for our example,

$$t = \frac{4.75 - 9.0}{5.34/\sqrt{20-1}} = \frac{-4.25}{1.22}$$

$$= -3.48$$

To use this figure we must have already chosen a level of significance, say 0.005. The meaning of t is then established by reference to a table of t values. One of these tables is reproduced in Appendix 5. As you will see, the top row indicates the level of significance required. The first column, however, introduces a new element, *df or degrees of freedom*. The precise meaning of degrees of freedom need not detain you: suffice to say that for values of t, df is always equal to the number of cases in the sample minus one (df = N−1). So here we read across the row of 19 degrees of freedom until we reach the column for 0.005 significance, and we find that the value is 2.861. The interpretation is simple: if the value of t which we calculated is the same as or greater than the value in our table then we can reject the null hypothesis. If it is less than the value in the table then we are not in a position to reject the null hypothesis. In other words our research hypothesis may be erroneous and further testing will be necessary. For our example a value of t = −3.48 is greater than the value required at this level of significance. We can therefore reject the null hypothesis and accept the research hypothesis that the population mean for this variable is less than nine years.

Summary

Social scientists utilize inductive statistics in order to assess the characteristics of a population from the characteristics of a sample drawn from it. The size, construction and composition of a sample will determine how well or badly it represents the population from which it is drawn. All samples contain *error* attributable to the inevitable difference between the sample and the population, but this can be allowed for in statistical measurement. What the researcher is more directly responsible for is the control of *bias*, unrepresentativeness of the sample which is attributable to poor design or execution of the sampling procedure itself.

Statistical tests associated with sampling rely on the theory of distribution curves for their capacity to estimate parameters of the population from statistics of the sample. As well as the normal

distribution another important distribution curve, Student's 't' distribution is commonly used. This distribution, and the test based upon
it, allows the researcher to test hypotheses about the population,
using even very small samples.

Further exercises

A Using a random numbers table, take another sample of 89 cases from the
database. Create a new computer file for this second sample.

B Calculate the mean and standard deviation of the variables 'age' and
'service' for your new sample data. How do they compare with the first
sample? How do they compare with the population parameter?

Notes

1 W.J. Reichmann, *Use and Abuse of Statistics* (Harmondsworth, Pelican
Books, 1964), p. 245.
2 C. O'Muircheartraigh and D.P. Francis, *Statistics. A Dictionary of Terms and
Ideas* (London, Arrow Books, 1981).
3 W.M. Harper, *Statistics* (3rd edn, Plymouth, Macdonald and Evans, 1977),
p. 160.

7 Working with Two Variables

So far in this book we have dealt with the characteristics of samples and populations in terms of single, individual variables only. Chapters 4 and 5 showed how to order, describe and summarize variables by the use of frequency distribution, measures of dispersion and visual representation. Chapter 6 explained how the theory of sampling permits us to use a sample as the basis for generalization about a larger population. At all times, however, we have been concerned with the values of any *one* variable – the mean average age, the ratio of men to women, the most common length of service. In social sciences we are frequently interested not just in the characteristics of a single variable but in the relationship between two variables in the same sample. This is what we term *bivariate analysis*.

7.1 Bivariate analysis

Many of the questions which the social scientist addresses involve the relationship between two (or more) variables. We are commonly required to try to explain variation in one variable by referring to the influence of a second variable. 'Is there a relationship between the rate of unemployment and the incidence of suicide?' would be just such a question. Or again, 'Does social class affect educational performance?' I introduced, in chapter 3, section 3.4, the concept of *dependent* and *independent variables*, the latter being the *explanatory variable* which determines the variation in the former. In our questions above, the rate of unemployment would be the independent variable, the rate of suicide the dependent; social class the independent, educational performance the dependent. Variation in the independent variable helps to explain variation in the dependent variable.

On the face of it bivariate analysis is the investigation of *causality*: our questions might be rephrased, 'Does an increase in unemployment cause an increase in the incidence of suicide?' or 'Does low social class cause poor educational performance?' However, although our enquiries are certainly of this nature, the strict causal model of explanation is not deemed appropriate for social sciences. There are three basic reasons for this:

(1) Studying sociological variables normally means studying the behaviour and characteristics of people, or of organizations and groups established and perpetuated by people. What causes human behaviour is a complex and sometimes unanswerable question: we should not expect to find in the social sciences the kind of clear-cut relationship of cause and effect sometimes (though not always) obtainable in the natural sciences. Instead we are always talking in terms not of certainty but of *probability*. Rather than talk about causality we talk about *association* between variables. In other words, we aspire only to establish that an association exists between two variables in a sample and to analyse the nature and strength of that association.

(2) In any relationship between sociological variables an often large and complex pattern of influences will be at work. In attempting to establish a relationship between two variables we must always be alive to the possibility that one or more other variables may also be influencing the relationship. This is examined in greater depth in the following chapter in which we consider *multivariate analysis*. Suffice to say here that outcomes in the social world tend not to be easily attributable to a single influence. For example, the relationship between unemployment and suicide may be complicated by factors such as age (e.g. the two rates only increase together for certain age groups and not others) or marital status (e.g. single unemployed people do seem more prone to suicide but married unemployed people do not).

(3) It is not always clear which variable is dependent and which independent. That is, we do not know the *direction* of the relationship. In many cases direction is obvious from common sense (suicide is unlikely to determine unemployment) but this is not invariably so. Attitudinal variables are a good case in point. Say, for example, a researcher studying racial attitudes finds that

people who regularly work with employees of different ethnic origins have more tolerant racial attitudes than those who work in jobs where there are no other racial groups. The first temptation would be to cite the work environment as the independent variable and attitude as the dependent (i.e. working with other ethnic groups makes people more tolerant of them), but this might not be correct. It might be, for instance, that people with strong racist views consciously select jobs where they don't have to work alongside different racial groups (i.e. attitude to race influences selection of work environment). Here the direction of the association between the variables is by no means clear-cut. The researcher would have to investigate this relationship in more depth in order to establish its actual nature.

The statistical procedures used in bivariate analysis are designed to show us the probability or likelihood that an association exists between any two variables. They can also show the strength of that association. However, it is better to be too sceptical than too trusting: measures of association can at best provide good indications of the likelihood of a causal relationship in specific circumstances. *Statistics constitute a mathematically grounded guidance, never an incontrovertible proof.*

7.2 Association between two variables: (1) nominal level

The statistical procedure which we use to analyse the relationship between variables is, to some degree, determined by the level of measurement of the variables concerned. There are techniques available for interval level variables which cannot be used with nominal level ones, for instance. Certain techniques are generally applicable and the most common of these will be the subject of this section: *contingency tables.*

A *contingency table* is a tabular representation of the relationship between two variables. Very simply, it shows the pairs of values taken by each case in a sample or population for any two variables. Table 7.1 shows a contingency table for the two variables 'grade' and 'gender'. The table is divided into *cells*. Each cell represents the coincidence of a specific value from each variable. In this table there are eight cells and we refer to the size of contingency tables according to the number of *rows* and *columns* they have: this is a four by two table. In statistical computer programs a contingency table is normally referred to as a *cross-tabulation* of one variable by another: this is a cross-tabulation of grade by gender. It should also be noted

Table 7.1 *Cross-tabulation of grade by gender*

Gradgp	Count row PCT col PCT tot PCT	Gender Male 0.	Female 1.	Row Total
1.		57 27.8 31.0 16.0	148 72.2 86.0 41.6	205 57.6
2.		63 77.8 34.2 17.7	18 22.2 10.5 5.1	81 22.8
3.		19 76.0 10.3 5.3	6 24.0 3.5 1.7	25 7.0
4.		45 100.0 24.5 12.6	0 0.0 0.0 0.0	45 12.6
	Column Total	184 51.7	172 48.3	356 100.0

Chi square = 116.88343 with 3 degrees of freedom   Significance = 0.0000
Cramer's V = 0.57300
Number of missing observations = 1

that it is quite common (but by no means necessary) for the dependent variable to be written first and appear on the left-hand (rows) side of the table. This is because we may be cross-tabulating one dependent variable by a series of possible explanatory variables in order to compare the relationships or strength of association. In an instruction to a computer program such as SPSS we would write 'grade by gender, age, service' and the computer would produce one table for each of those cross-tabulations (grade by gender, grade by age, and so on).

The first step in analysing a contingency table is to look at the row, column and total percentages. These are given in each cell and at the side of the table. We can understand this by examining the table in detail. The left-hand side of the table shows the values of the variable 'grade'. Here, grade is represented as 'Gradgp' (grade grouped) because these are the grouped or aggregated values, and there are four categories: 1 (clerical and other grades); 2 (administrative and technical grades); 3 (senior officer grade); 4 (principal officer). The top of the table shows the two values of the variable 'gender', and these are labelled 0 (male) and 1 (female). On the right hand side of the table there are the row totals and row percentages. These figures indicate what number and percentage of cases are in each category of 'Gradgp' – that is, they represent a frequency distribution. We can see, for example, that 205 respondents were in category 1 and that this constituted 57.6 per cent of all of the cases. Below the table similar figures are given for 'gender': the total number and percentage in each category. For example, 172 respondents were female and this number constituted 48.3 per cent of all of the cases. At the bottom right hand corner of the table there is the total number of cases in the sample or population being used and the figure 100 per cent. Note that here there are 356 rather than 357 cases: for some reason, perhaps an error when the data were being put into the computer, the values for one case have not been recorded. This is not uncommon, but if there were to be a large number of missing cases this would have to be investigated and corrected. Note that on the last printed line the computer has informed us of this by stating that there is one missing 'observation'.

Now that we have established the information in what are sometimes called the margins of the table, we can look at the cells themselves. Take the very first cell of the table, the one in the top left hand corner. This reads:

	0
1.	57
	27.8
	31.0
	16.0

and represents all of the cases taking the value 0 for 'gender' and 1 for 'grade'. That is, it contains all of the *male clerical workers* in the survey. The first figure gives the actual number or frequency of these cases – 57 in the population as a whole. The second figure is a *row* percentage and shows *the percentage of clerical workers who are male*. The next figure is a *column* percentage and shows the *percentage of men who are clerical workers*. It is important to get this distinction clear: 27.8 per cent of clerical workers are men; 31.0 per cent of men are clerical workers. Finally, the bottom figure represents the percentage of all cases who are male clerical workers – 16.0 per cent.

Analysis of cell percentages should always be the first stage in reading contingency tables and, in some instances, this will be all that is required. A great deal can be discovered about the relationship between two variables simply by considering and comparing percentages. In table 7.1 our main interest will be whether 'gender' has any influence on 'grade'. By examining the table we will seek to establish whether there is any discernible pattern of association between being male or female and occupying a particular grade in the organization. As a reasonable working hypothesis we might suggest that women will occupy lower grades, in general, than men. Using the model of the null hypothesis (see chapter 6) we can approach our table with the assumption that 'grade' will not differ according to the respondent's gender: if it appears to, then perhaps our working hypothesis is indeed correct.

To begin such an analysis we can look at the row percentages for each grade: these reveal what proportions of each grade are male or female. The respective row percentages for each grade are:

	Male	Female
1 (clerical)	27.8	72.2
2 (admin.)	77.8	22.2
3 (senior officer)	76.0	24.0
4 (principal officer)	100.0	0.0

An immediate pattern should be evident even on first inspection. Women constitute almost three-quarters of the clerical grades but this proportion is reversed for both the administrative and the higher professional (senior officer) grades. In the highest, predominantly managerial, grade of principal officer there are no women at all. The absence of women from the top jobs and the striking contrast of the percentages in Grade 1 and Grades 2 and 3 encourages us to reject the assumption that gender has no influence on grade and to accept instead our initial hypothesis that women will occupy lower grades.

This first analysis can be extended by looking at the column percentages and considering what proportion of each sex is in each grade.

	Male	Female
1	31.0	86.0
2	34.2	10.5
3	10.3	3.5
4	24.5	0.0

Here, the occupation of the lower grades by women can be seen reflected in the very high proportion of women who are located in the clerical and related grades. This is in contrast to the much more even distribution of male workers across the grades. Whereas about a third of men are in clerical grades (31.0 per cent) another third in admin. grades (34.2 per cent) and a final third divided between the higher professional and managerial grades (10.3 and 24.5 per cent), the vast majority (86.0 per cent) of women are in grade category 1, with small percentages in 2 and 3. Not only, then, are most clerks women, but most women are clerks. A final illustration of the same point can be made by considering the total percentages, in particular that for the second cell, female clerical workers. This group constitutes 41.6 per cent of the total population. It is by far the largest single group (the next largest being male admin. staff, making up 17.7 per cent of the total) and, as such, constitutes a significant minority of all the cases in the population.

We can also use analysis of percentages to make more precise statements about possible relationships between the variables. Our initial examination of the figures suggests that gender is associated with grade inasmuch as women are concentrated in lower-grade categories than men. To be more exact we need to ask what the distribution of men and women across the grades would be *if there were no relationship between the variables*. We can see from the column totals that men represent 51.7 per cent of the population and women 48.3 per cent. If gender was having no influence on grade then, logically, each grade category should include the same proportion of men and women as the sample as a whole. In short, men should constitute 51.7 per cent of each category. If we take category 2 as an example, we see that there are 81 employees on the grades in this category. If men and women were distributed proportionately there would be 43 men (51.7 per cent of 81) and 39 women (48.3 per cent of 81) in this category. These figures were referred to as *expected frequencies*. In fact, there are 63 men and 18 women in category 2 and these are the actual or *observed frequencies*. Where there is a large or systematic difference in the expected and the observed frequencies then we may assume that there is some association between the two variables.

The difference between the observed and expected frequencies is the basis for the most commonly used statistical test connected with contingency tables. This is called the *chi-square test of significance* (represented by the Greek letter χ^2 pronounced 'ki'). The chi-square test measures all of the differences between observed and expected frequencies in a table and provides a chi-square value for the table. In itself this value tells us very little as its magnitude is effected by the number of cells in the table. We utilize it in combination with a table of chi-square values which indicates at what level the value is *statistically significant*. We met the concept of statistical significance in chapter 6, but it might be useful to refresh our memories here. Put very simply, statistical significance is a measure of probability; it tells us how likely it is that an observed value or association has occurred purely by chance. The higher the level of statistical significance, the lower the likelihood that the value is the outcome of a chance distribution of values and the higher the likelihood that our value is a reliable indicator. You will recall that a 0.05 level of significance was equivalent to a 95 per cent level of confidence – five chances in 100 of being mistaken; a 0.01 level represented one chance in 100; and a 0.001 level, one chance in 1,000. Which level we select depends on the size of the sample being measured and on our own requirements of accuracy.

For any contingency table a value of chi-square can be produced and the level of significance of this figure established. For the smallest size of contingency table possible (a 2 × 2, four-cell table) it is usual not to use chi-square but a similar measure, phi-square (ϕ^2) specially designed to deal with small contingency tables. A glance at our cross tabulation of 'grade' and 'gender' shows that the chi-square value for the table is 116.88343. The computer program also automatically indicates the level of significance: here it is 0.0000, suggesting that the relationship is significant at a level higher than the $p = 0.001$ which we would normally require. However, in Appendix 5 there is a table of chi-square values and you will see that it can be read in the same way as the table of t values discussed in chapter 6. Along the top row there are levels of significance; down the first column there are degrees of freedom. These are a control for the effect of the size of the table and in chi-square tests the number of degrees of freedom can be discovered by a simple procedure. If we ignore the bottom row and the final column of a contingency table, then count the remaining cells, the number of cells is also the degrees of freedom. So, for example in our table, there are three degrees of freedom. In, say, a four by three table there will be six degrees of freedom. To find the level of significance simply read across the row of the appropriate degrees of freedom until a figure the same as or greater than your chi-square value is located. Read up this column to find the level of significance.

The value of chi-square and its level of statistical significance can only indicate whether or not an association between two variables is likely to exist. If the chi-square value is statistically significant at an acceptable level then other statistics must be used to measure the *strength* of the relationship. These are called *measures of association* and there are different measures connected with different types of statistical tests and different levels of measurement. For our purposes here just one, fairly common measure has been used in association with chi-square and this is called *Cramer's V*. Like most other measures of association Cramer's V provides a value on a range from 0 to 1 where zero represents *no association* between the variables and one represents *perfect association* (one variable predicting the value of the other totally). In simple terms the nearer to 1 that the value reaches, the stronger the relationship between the variables. It is not possible to define precisely what is a weak or strong value of Cramer's V as the value needs to be read in conjunction with the chi-square test of significance and, ideally, in comparison with measures of other relationships. However, the value of Cramer's V for our grade by gender table is 0.57300 which, in conjunction with a chi-square significance level of 0.001 suggests that we can be confident that a fairly strong relationship exists between an employee's gender and her/his grade level.

It is unlikely that in a real-life piece of research we would be interested only in one isolated table. Commonly the greatest use of measures such as chi-square and Cramer's V is in the comparison of relationships between a group of variables. Table 7.2, for instance, shows another cross-tabulation from the same data – 'grade' (represented as grouped categories) against 'age' (also grouped). As with the previous table, we are interested in whether a relationship exists between the variables, and more particularly, whether we can detect that an employee's age influences her/his grade. As this is a much larger, four by six, table with 24 cells, percentage analysis is more cumbersome and calculation of observed and expected frequencies would be extremely time-consuming. A consideration of the chi-square values and the values of Cramer's V provides us with an easier comparison.

The chi-square value of 80.08864 is significant at greater than 0.001. Note that the magnitude of the chi-square value is not of

Table 7.2 Cross tabulation of 'grade' (grouped) by 'age' (grouped)

Gradgp	Count / row PCT / col PCT / tot PCT	Agegrp 1. 16–20yrs	2. 21–30yrs	3. 31–40yrs	4. 41–50yrs	5. 51–60yrs	6. 61 and over	Row total
1.	Count	40	69	22	35	38	1	205
	row PCT	19.5	33.7	10.7	17.1	18.5	0.5	57.4
	col PCT	85.1	72.6	32.8	49.3	55.9	11.1	
	tot PCT	11.2	19.3	6.2	9.8	10.6	0.3	
2.	Count	5	17	21	15	19	4	81
	row PCT	6.2	21.0	25.9	18.5	23.5	4.9	22.7
	col PCT	10.6	17.9	31.3	21.1	17.9	44.4	
	tot PCT	1.4	4.8	5.9	4.2	5.3	1.1	
3.	Count	2	9	8	2	5	0	26
	row PCT	7.7	34.6	30.8	7.7	19.2	0.0	7.3
	col PCT	4.3	9.5	11.9	2.8	7.4	0.0	
	tot PCT	0.6	2.5	2.2	0.6	1.4	0.0	
4.	Count	0	0	16	19	6	4	45
	row PCT	0.0	0.0	35.6	42.2	13.3	8.9	12.6
	col PCT	0.0	0.0	23.9	26.8	8.8	44.4	
	tot PCT	0.0	0.0	4.5	5.3	1.7	1.1	
Column total		47	95	67	71	68	9	357
		13.2	26.6	18.8	19.9	19.0	2.5	100.0

6 out of 24 (25.0%) of the valid cells have expected cell frequency less than 5.0
Minimum expected cell frequency = 0.655
Chi square = 80.08864 with 15 degrees of freedom   significance = 0.0000
Cramer's V = 0.27346

direct importance: we would expect a much larger table to produce a larger value of chi-square. What matters is the level of significance. The value of Cramer's V is 0.27346 noticeably lower than for the previous table and this certainly suggests that the relationship between grade and age is weaker than that between grade and gender. Of course all three variables are likely to be interrelated and in chapter 8 we will see how they can be assessed together. For the present, our measurement of contingency tables has allowed us to investigate the nature, direction and strength of relationships between our variables.

Because the analysis of contingency tables can take the simple form of percentage analysis, and because its related measures are based on the difference between observed and expected frequencies, it is a suitable vehicle for the investigation of relationships at all levels of measurement. It is used most often with nominal and ordinal level variables, partly because more sophisticated measures exist for interval level data, but also because the large number of possible values occurring with an interval variable would produce an unmanageably large table. Interval level variables are normally converted into ordinal variables by aggregating the values into ordered categories (as with 'age' in our example) before analysis in a contingency table. In the following sections we will introduce other measures specifically designed to analyse relationships between two ordinal or two interval level variables. However, many of the principles encountered in this section will remain relevant, particularly the interpretation of measures of association.

7.3 Association between two variables: (2) ordinal level

At the ordinal level of measurement the values of a variable are ranked, i.e. arranged in an hierarchical order. We can take advantage of this ranking in the measurement of association between two ordinal variables. There are two correlation statistics which are based on a comparison of the position of cases on ranked scales of values: these are referred to as statistics of *rank-order correlation*. Both measures are named after their originators with the suffix of a Greek letter: there is *Spearman's ρ (rho)*, also known as Spearman's coefficient of rank order correlation; and *Kendall's τ (tau)*.

Both of these measures demonstrate the *strength* of the relationship between the two variables and are measured on a scale from −1 to +1. This is similar to the measures of association connected with contingency tables, where 0 represented *no association* between the variables and 1 represented *perfect association*. However, with ordinal and interval variables we have two forms of perfect association – perfect *positive* association (+1) and perfect *negative* association (−1). This is possible because once we have an order to the values then the distribution of the variables can vary in different directions. Either variable A can increase as variable B increases, or variable A can decrease as variable B increases. Where the two distributions increase identically together then there is perfect positive association; where one variable decreases in direct relation to the increase of the other variable then there is perfect negative association. The coefficient produced by the correlation expresses the *direction* as well as the strength of the relationship. So a value of −7.0, for example, would suggest a strong negative relationship (i.e. as one variable increases so the other one decreases); a value of +4.6 would suggest a fairly weak, positive association (as one variable increases so the other also increases but by no means identically).

Let us take an example of two ordinal variables which we might reasonably expect to be associated: 'grade' and 'length of service'. Here we are using 'service' in its aggregated form and so it constitutes an ordinal variable ranging from the category 'less than one year's service' (1) to '20 years and more' (7); the variable 'grade' has again been recoded slightly so that the 'other' category (which includes predominantly secretarial and similar grades) is combined with the clerical (1) category. If we imagine all of the cases in the population as a series of paired values (the value of 'grade' and the value of 'service'), then the association between the variables derives from the similarity or difference between the values in each of these pairs. This will be represented statistically in a single coefficient.

The two measures are in fact derived in slightly different ways and, consequently, produce different values for the same relationship. Spearman's *rho* is calculated by taking the difference on the rank positions of each pair of values and manipulating these differences (the precise formula need not concern us here), whereas Kendall's *tau* is based on the extent to which one set of ranked values would have to be changed to agree with the other set. In other words, where Spearman's is based on the *difference* of each *pair* of ranked values, Kendall's derives from the difference between the *order* of the two *sets* of values. In practice, the main disparity between the two is that Kendall's tends to produce a slightly lower figure for the same association. Spearman's is possibly the better

Table 7.3 *Rank order correlation (two measures) for two pairs of ordinal variables*

Spearman Correlation Coefficients

Variable pair		Variable pair	
Gradgp	0.3558	Gradgp	0.2597
with	N(357)	with	N(357)
servgp	SIG .001	Agegrp	SIG .001

Kendall Correlation Coefficients

Variable pair		Variable pair	
Gradgp	0.2954	Gradgp	0.2205
with	N(357)	with	N(357)
servgp	SIG .001	Agegrp	SIG .001

known in social statistics but both are readily available on computer programs for correlation procedures.

For our correlation of 'grade' with 'service' the rank-order correlation produces a value for Spearman's *rho* of $r^s = 0.3558$, and a value for Kendall's *tau* of $\tau = 0.2954$. Both figures indicate a positive, but fairly weak, association. We can also measure the level of significance of this figure and both are significant at the 0.001 level. Table 7.3 shows computer printout with details of both measurements. As with other measures of association rank-order correlation can be at its most useful in the comparison of relationships between connected variables. Table 7.3 also shows rank-order correlation coefficients for the relationship between 'age' (grouped into ranked categories) and 'grade'. As is immediately obvious, although the coefficients for this latter relationship are still statistically significant, they are, on both measures, smaller than for the previous relationship. Our tentative interpretation for this would be that although neither service nor age are strongly associated with grade, the former has more influence than the latter; an employee's length of service, in other words, is a better predictor of her/his grade position than is her/his age.

7.4 Association between two variables: (3) interval level

Most of the measures used to represent the relationship between variables at the interval level of measurement are expressed in a form similar to the measures of association or *correlation coefficients* encountered in our study of nominal and ordinal variables. Because, however, we are dealing with variables which have mathematically calculable values, any association can be measured with greater accuracy, and there exists a larger range of measures available for interval level variables. In this chapter we will look only at some of the simplest and most commonly used of these: techniques which normally come under the heading of *linear regression*.

The starting point for understanding the techniques of linear regression is a simple diagram called the *scattergram* or *scatter-plot*. This is simply a graph with one variable represented on the vertical (Y) axis, and the other variable represented on the horizontal (X) axis. In this graph each case is plotted at one point on the scattergram at the place where the appropriate values for the two variables coincide. The completed diagram consists of a 'scatter' of points representing the distribution of the cases between the possible values.

The scatter of points on a scattergram represents the relationship between the two variables being measured. When the points are very widely scattered and form no obvious pattern, then there is no systematic relationship between the variables: an apparently random distribution of points expresses the random coincidence of values between the two variables and the absence of any correlation. The more obviously the points are clustered together, and form a discernible pattern, the more likely it is that a relationship exists. One simple way of illustrating this is to try to draw a line through the scatter of points so that the line approximates the pattern made by the points. Obviously, the more closely and uniformly clustered the points are, the easier this will be. Figure 5.1 shows possible scattergrams for three types of relationship between two variables. In each scattergram a line has been added to represent the relationship.

Assuming that our scattergram permits us to draw a reasonable line to represent the points, how do we then interpret the line? Recalling our assumption that an entirely random scatter meant no relationship existed, we can argue that the closer the points fall to the line, the stronger the correlation between the variables. We can

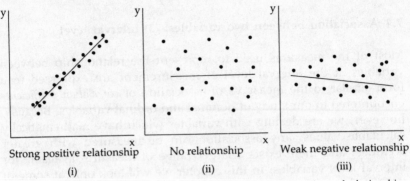

Figure 7.1 *Scattergrams showing different strengths and directions of relationships between variables*

also interpret the direction of the line. A line which slopes upward from left to right on the graph represents a relationship in which the values of the dependent variable (Y) increase as the values of the independent variable (X) increase: we call this *positive association*. Conversely, a line which slopes downward from left to right represents a relationship in which the values of the variable on the Y axis decline as the values of the variable on the X axis increase: a case of *negative association*. The line through the data points does not have to be a straight line, although it is straight line relationships which mostly concern the social scientist. A scatter of data might be best represented by a curved line and this too can be interpreted in terms of the relationship between the variables.

Although the general principles of observation remain the same, these 'rule of thumb' type of interpretations of scattergrams can be improved by the use of accurate statistical measures. Firstly, we can improve the line drawn through the points by constructing a line calculated mathematically. This is called the *line of best fit* and is based on the idea of minimizing the vertical distance between each point and a line drawn through them: the calculation of this line is called *least-squares regression*. A line which best fits the pattern of the scattergram will most accurately represent the relationship between the variables, and this line is also referred to as a *regression line*, hence the general term 'linear regression' for the procedures involved in correlating interval variables in this way.

Producing a mathematically calculated regression line enables us to further improve our description of the relationship represented in the scattergram. Using the calculations made in the least-squares procedure we can produce a single figure which expresses the 'goodness of fit' of the line: this is called the *Pearson product-moment correlation coefficient*, more simply symbolized as r. Like other coefficients, r has a range of values from −1 to +1 in which −1 represents perfect negative association, +1 perfect positive association, and 0 represents no systematic linear association. Interpretation of this figure therefore provides both the *strength* and *direction* of the relationship: a low negative value, for example, would represent a weak inverse relationship and would be expressed as a downward sloping line with many of the points fairly well dispersed from the regression line. A high positive value would, on the other hand, represent a strong linear relationship and would be expressed by a regression line rising from left to right, with the majority of points on, or clustered close to, the line. Figure 7.2 shows three possible values of r for different relationships plotted on scattergrams.

It seems appropriate at this point to add a few words of warning about the interpretation of correlation coefficients in general. The first and most important advice is that these figures cannot be treated in a mechanical way as if their meaning was fixed and self-evident. Two regression lines may have the same correlation coefficient value yet may be rather different lines expressing quite different distributions of cases. Of course the measure of association is a guide and a form of comparison between relationships but it does not, by itself, define the *nature* of the relationship. Secondly, comparison of two values of r cannot be made on a strictly mathematical basis: an r value of 0.6 is not three times as strong as an r value of 0.2. Similarly, r values cannot be added together or otherwise manipulated mathematically: each describes a specific and unique relationship between two variables. As with our other

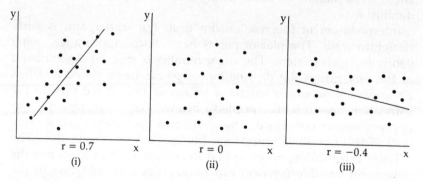

Figure 7.2 *Examples of Pearson's r values for scattergrams showing different relationships between variables*

measures of association for nominal and ordinal variables, the use of linear regression is a statistical evaluation of probability, a refinement on common sense, not an unequivocal proof.

To aid our interpretation of these statistical procedures one further statistic can be introduced – the *coefficient of determination*. This is represented as r^2 and is, mathematically, the correlation coefficient squared. Why is it of any use? The coefficient of determination is valuable because it represents the amount of variation explained by the regression of one variable on another. For example, in a regression of two variables, Y and X, we are interested in knowing how much of the variation in Y could be attributed to variation in X. Let us suppose that for that regression a value of 0.8 is produced for r^2. Very simply, this means that 80 per cent of the variation in the dependent variable can be explained by variation in the independent variable. This, by extension, means that 20 per cent of the variation in Y must be attributable to other factors – variables not included in the equation, perhaps. As this coefficient of determination is our correlation coefficient squared, it is obvious that to produce as large an r^2 as 0.8 will require an even larger value of r (in this case 0.89), which in itself will indicate a strong positive relationship.

Figure 7.3 shows the two interval level variables from our example database, 'age' and 'service', presented as a scattergram. Each asterisk represents one case and, where more than one case takes the same pair of values, the asterisk is replaced by the number of cases coinciding at that point. For some members of the population (e.g. young employees with short employment service) a large number of cases have the same characteristics. As the values for both 'age' and 'service' increase so the number of cases decreases and the likelihood of cases taking the same pair of values also diminishes.

Interpretation of the relationship from the scattergram is fairly straightforward. The plot of points has a linear appearance, rising gently from left to right. The larger number of cases at the left hand of the plot makes the distribution of points more varied and less obviously linear where length of service is low. If we turn to the correlation coefficients printed below the scattergram, our impressions are confirmed. The correlation coefficient r has a value of 0.53260, a positive correlation but not a very strong one. The value of r^2 is 0.28366, meaning that 28 per cent of the variation in the dependent variable (service) can be explained by variation in the independent variable (age). Again this indicates a level of association between the variables which would require consideration in

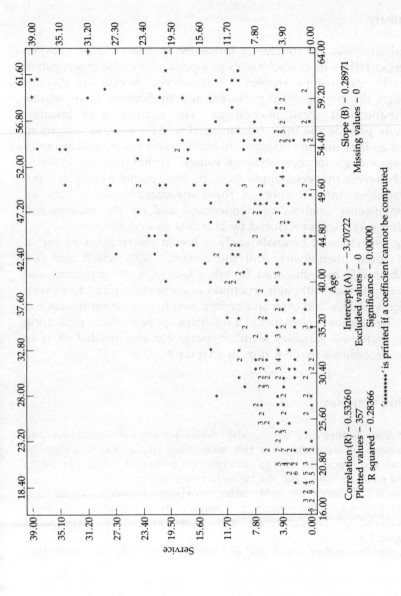

Figure 7.3 Scattergram of the variables 'age' and 'service'

Correlation (R) — 0.53260
Plotted values — 357
R squared — 0.28366

Intercept (A) — −3.70722
Excluded values — 0
Significance — 0.00000

Slope (B) — 0.28971
Missing values — 0

'********' is printed if a coefficient cannot be computed

constructing analyses of the data, but also indicates a substantial amount of variation explained by other variables.

Summary

Social scientists are commonly interested in relationships between different factors or characteristics of a population. The investigation of such relationships enables the researcher to evaluate theories through the testing of hypotheses, and to develop more reliable explanations of social phenomena. The techniques of bivariate analysis provide the most fundamental tool for such investigation, based as they are on statistical probability and the measurement of the association or correlation of values. Techniques are available which have a universal application, or one specific to certain types of variables: interpretation of these measures depends both on common-sense analysis of frequencies, and on the various correlation coefficients produced by bivariate procedures.

The weakness of bivariate analysis lies in the complex nature of most social phenomena, and the certainty with which any two variables will be influenced by other factors, both important and relatively trivial. Although repetition of correlation procedures with related variables and extensive comparison of correlation figures can limit the unknown elements in a relationship, procedures measuring more than two variables simultaneously are also needed. It is to these procedures that we turn in chapter 8.

Further exercises

A Produce contingency tables, with values for level of significance and strength of association, for two more cross-tabulations: 'Gradegp' by 'Servgp'; 'gender' by 'Servgp'. Interpret the tables and statistics produced and compare them with the tables in this chapter.

B Produce statistics for rank order correlation between 'Agegp' and 'Servgp', using Spearman's r. Compare these statistics with those produced for the scattergram of the same two variables *ungrouped* in figure 7.3.

C Repeat the scattergram of 'age' and 'service' using only the sample data.

8 Working with Three or More Variables

I have stated on a number of occasions during this introduction to statistics that the nature of sociological variables, their distribution and relationships, are complex and resistant to simple, monocausal explanation. It is not surprising, then, that statisticians have developed techniques for measuring complex relationships between a number of variables, and that these have been eagerly utilized by social researchers. Indeed such techniques, grouped together under the heading *multivariate analysis,* have constituted the primary growth area of social statistics in the past 30 years as social scientists have attempted to enhance their analytic capabilities through refinements of statistical technique. Much of this subject area lies beyond the scope of this book and has been dealt with in detail elsewhere, but the purpose of this chapter is to introduce a small number of important statistical procedures in the field of multivariate analysis which should be accessible to the relative novice.

The main problem which multivariate analysis attempts to solve is that of discriminating between possible explanatory variables in terms of their influence on a single dependent variable. We have mentioned some of the difficulties created by the complex nature of social causality but hitherto we have been dealing with only two variables in the simplest of relationships. This can be summarized diagrammatically as:

Variable A ⟶ Variable B

where the arrow represents the direction of influence. Once, however, we introduce the possibility of more than two variables, the nature of the relationship becomes less simple. Let us take two examples of three-variable relationships. In the first the *apparent* association between variable A and variable B is in fact due to both of these variables being primarily influenced by a third factor, C.

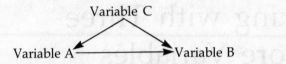

An example of such a relationship would be the association between earnings and trade union membership, where both would, in fact, be primarily determined by a third factor, occupation.

An alternative arrangement is that characterized by the *intervening* variable, thus:

Variable A ————————►Variable C ————————►Variable B

Here, on first analysis, A and B *appear* to be associated. However, when other explanatory variables are included in the model, it becomes clear that A only effects B through the intermediary factor C: A influences C; C influences B. An example of this would be gender and earnings. At first sight gender would seem to be closely associated with level of earnings. However, this association is only achieved through the effect of gender on occupation: in other words, it is the relative access to occupational status which primarily differentiates women's and men's pay.

Evidently, in sociological research, explanations can only be confidently constructed after possibilities such as the above have been properly assessed. It is common to find the situation in which a number of variables exist as possible explanations of a single dependent variable but where the precise relationship between them is not immediately clear. In such a situation the researcher must first use common sense to evaluate the likely associations, bearing in mind the *time sequence* of variables (e.g. a variable 'home-ownership' is unlikely to influence 'occupation' as the former is normally chronologically consequent upon the latter), and the *proximity* of their relationship (e.g. 'religious belief' may be associated with 'occupation', and may even influence it, but only through a complex of intervening attitudinal variables). Having made some cautious assumptions about the structure of relationships involved, statistical procedures can be employed to assess these more accurately.

8.1 Contingency tables using controlled variables

The simplest method of analysing multivariate relationships, and one which is applicable to all levels of measurement, is the use of contingency tables with *controlled variables*. To control for a variable means that *the value of that variable is held constant in the presence of other variables*. If, for example, a researcher is trying to explain the variation in a variable C, and has two main possible explanatory variables, A and B, then the association between A and C can be measured holding B constant; subsequently, the reverse can be done. In practice, holding an independent variable constant means measuring the association between A and C for every possible value of B. So, if variable B has four values, four measures will be taken. Using contingency tables this can be very simply illustrated.

Let us take as our example the relationship between 'service' and 'grade', but this time with the addition of a third variable, 'gender'. 'Grade' here is the dependent variable and both 'service' and 'gender' are possible explanatory variables: we already know that length of service is associated with grade level, but we now wish to know whether this association varies according to the gender of the employee. We control for the variable 'gender' by producing a contingency table of the association between 'grade' and 'service' for each of the values of the variable 'gender'. As there are only two possible values this procedure is comparatively simple: a contingency table is produced for male employees only, followed by a contingency table for female employees only. These tables are shown as table 8.1 and 8.2. The interpretation of these tables is quite straightforward. If an employee's sex had no influence on her/his grade *and* if length of service did not vary significantly according to gender, then we would expect the two tables to be more or less the same. If, in fact, gender is associated with both grade and service, then controlling for the effect of gender will allow us to isolate, to some degree, its influence on the other two variables. Let us look more closely at the table to illustrate this.

Table 8.1 is a cross-tabulation of 'grade' and 'service' (both in their grouped form – Gradgp, Servgp) for male employees only. The heading of the table indicates that the procedure is 'controlling for gender' and the first value of the variable 'gender' is O.male. A first consideration of the table suggests that men are distributed across the grade levels with relatively little influence from their length of service. The only immediately noticeable area is the pair of cells in

Table 8.1 Cross-tabulation controlling for a third variable: grade by service by gender (male)

	Servgp								
Gradgp	Up to 1 year 0.	1 – 2 yrs 1.	2 – 4 yrs 2.	4 – 6 yrs 3.	6 – 10 yrs 4.	10 – 15 yrs 5.	15 – 20 yrs 6.	20 years and over 7.	Row total
Count / row PCT / col PCT / tot PCT									
1.	11 / 19.3 / 57.9 / 6.0	7 / 12.3 / 50.0 / 3.8	4 / 7.0 / 26.7 / 2.2	16 / 28.1 / 43.2 / 8.7	11 / 19.3 / 33.3 / 6.0	8 / 14.0 / 27.6 / 4.3	0 / 0.0 / 0.0 / 0.0	0 / 0.0 / 0.0 / 0.0	57 / 31.0
2.	3 / 4.8 / 15.8 / 1.6	3 / 4.8 / 21.4 / 1.6	3 / 4.8 / 20.0 / 1.6	10 / 15.9 / 27.0 / 5.4	13 / 20.6 / 39.4 / 7.1	10 / 15.9 / 34.5 / 5.4	6 / 9.5 / 66.7 / 3.3	15 / 23.8 / 53.6 / 8.2	63 / 34.2
3.	1 / 5.3 / 5.3 / 0.5	0 / 0.0 / 0.0 / 0.0	5 / 26.3 / 33.3 / 2.7	3 / 15.8 / 8.1 / 1.6	3 / 15.8 / 9.1 / 1.6	2 / 10.5 / 6.9 / 1.1	0 / 0.0 / 0.0 / 0.0	5 / 26.3 / 17.9 / 2.7	10.3
4.	4 / 8.9 / 21.1 / 2.2	4 / 8.9 / 28.6 / 2.2	3 / 6.7 / 20.0 / 1.6	8 / 17.8 / 21.6 / 4.3	6 / 13.3 / 18.2 / 3.3	9 / 20.0 / 31.0 / 4.9	3 / 6.7 / 33.3 / 1.6	8 / 17.8 / 28.6 / 4.3	45 / 24.5
Column total	19 / 10.3	14 / 7.6	15 / 8.2	37 / 20.1	33 / 17.9	29 / 15.8	9 / 4.9	28 / 15.2	184 / 100.0

Cramer's V = 0.28319

Table 8.2 *Cross-tabulation controlling for a third variable (second value): grade by service by gender (female)*

Gradgp	Servgp	0. Up to 1 year	1. 1-2 yrs	2. 2-4 yrs	3. 4-6 yrs	4. 6-10 yrs	5. 10-15 yrs	6. 15-20 yrs	7. 20 years and over	Row total
	Count / row PCT / col PCT / tot PCT									
1.		22	26	14	51	30	5	0	0	148
		14.9	17.6	9.5	34.5	20.3	3.4	0.0	0.0	86.0
		95.7	86.7	87.5	87.9	93.8	62.5	0.0	0.0	
		12.8	15.1	8.1	29.7	17.4	2.9	0.0	0.0	
2.		1	1	1	5	2	3	1	4	18
		5.6	5.6	5.6	27.8	11.1	16.7	5.6	22.2	10.5
		4.3	3.3	6.3	8.6	6.3	37.5	100.0	100.0	
		0.6	0.6	0.6	2.9	1.2	1.7	0.6	2.3	
3.		0	3	1	2	0	0	0	0	6
		0.0	50.0	16.7	33.3	0.0	0.0	0.0	0.0	3.5
		0.0	10.0	6.3	3.4	0.0	0.0	0.0	0.0	
		0.0	1.7	0.6	1.2	0.0	0.0	0.0	0.0	
Column total		23	30	16	58	32	8	1	4	172
		13.4	17.4	9.3	33.7	18.6	4.7	0.6	2.3	100.0

Cramer's V = 0.41363

the top right hand corner of the table where the absence of any cases indicates that no-one with 15 or more years service is still on a clerical grade. Looking at each row, that is at each grade, in turn we first see that, with the exception of the two cells already mentioned, there are male clerical workers with everything from less than a year to 15 years' service. In percentage terms these are spread out across the range of employment duration. In the second level of grades there is a more obvious clustering of cases in the mid- and long-service categories. Only 14 per cent of employees who had reached administrative grades had four or fewer years service whereas over 50 per cent had between four and 15 years, and 23.8 per cent (the largest single group) had over 20 years service. The number of employees in category three is much smaller and there is no strong pattern to the distribution: all but one employee had more than two years' service, but almost half (47.4 per cent, N=9) had six or fewer years with the organization. A similar pattern is evident for the higher professional and managerial category in which 42.3 per cent had less than six years' service, revealing a weak tendency for service to predict higher grade.

The interpretation of the table might begin by suggesting that service did have an influence on grade for male workers but that the influence was relatively weak. The grades included in category 2 seemed more closely tied to service than the higher grades and this might reflect the influence of professional recruitment for Grades 3 and 4 compared to internal promotion to Grade 2. Such an interpretation would be supported by the value for Cramer's V printed below the table which shows a relatively weak association (V = 0.28319).

Turning next to the cross-tabulation of the same variables for female employees only (table 8.2) we see some rather different patterns. Firstly, of course, there is no fourth row as there are no women on category 4 grades. In the first grade row we note that, as with the preceding table, there were no clerical workers with over 15 years' service and, again similar to the male employees, the largest category of workers in the lower grades were those with between four and six years service (34.5 per cent women, 28.1 per cent men). The small number of women in grade level 2 are fairly well dispersed but, in percentage terms, are again similar to the men: only three (16.8 per cent) had four or fewer years' service, 55.6 per cent had between four and ten years (compared with 52.4 per cent of men) and 22.2 per cent had 20 years or more (compared with 23.8 per cent of the men). So for these grades the relation between service and grade seems to be similar for both sexes. In category 3 there are only six women and all of these have under six years' service. These seem to parallel the fairly large proportions of men on grades 3 and 4 with relatively short service but the absence of long-service women in these categories and the complete absence of women from the higher grades renders further comparison difficult. How should we interpret the figures?

One obvious point to make is that, for whatever reason, women are not attaining high grades in any significant numbers. But, in the context of these tables, does their length of service have anything to do with it? If we look at the *column* percentages we can see that a very small proportion of women had long service with the organization. Only 7.6 per cent (N=13) of women had been with the organization over ten years, compared to 35.9 per cent (N=66) of the men. Given that length of service seems to have some effect on grade level, this discrepancy could be accounting for some of the discrepancy in grade between men and women. However, when we do compare groups of men and women with similar employment duration their fates appear quite different. The largest category for both sexes, in terms of service, is category 3 (four to six years) which includes 20.1 per cent of men and 33.7 per cent of women. However, using the column percentages in each table, we can see that whereas those male employees were well distributed across the grades, the women with comparable service were overwhelmingly concentrated in Grade 1, as the figures show:

4 up to 6 years' service

Grade	Men	Women	
1	43.2	87.9	
2	27.0	8.6	
3	8.1	3.4	
4	21.6	0.0	(all percentages)

A similar comparison can be made for those with six and up to ten years' service. This category includes almost identical proportions of each gender (17.9 per cent of men, 18.6 per cent of women) but their respective distributions are in stark contrast. The men are quite evenly dispersed with approximately one third on the lower (1), middle (2) and higher (3, 4) grades. Women, however, are, with the exception of two cases (6.3 per cent) located in the grade category 1.

Such use of both column, row and total percentages allows us to investigate the comparison between the sexes in some detail. We

might also note that the Cramer's V for the second table is larger
(V=0.41363) suggesting that the two variables are more closely
associated for female employees. However, it is likely, from what
we've already noted, that this is not a positive association. With the
exception of a small number of women in Grade 2, long service has
not produced a change in women's grade level – most remain
clerical workers. Indeed location in Grade 3, the highest attained by
women in the population, is associated with relatively short service.
Conclusions of this kind necessarily point the way to the influence
of other variables – qualification, age and training for example – and
the next step for the researcher in this instance would be to repeat
these procedures using other combinations of variables.

It should be evident from the example which we have followed
above that the device of controlling for variables using contingency
tables provides an extremely valuable method for exploring multivariate relationships while using relatively simple statistical procedures. It does, of course, have its limitations: large tables, or the
inclusion of further variables makes analysis significantly more
difficult; variables have to be treated with a limited number of
values, which rules out most interval level variables. In the next
section we shall look at an extension of another procedure first
encountered in chapter 7 – linear regression – to show how a
number of interrelated variables can be treated simultaneously.

8.2 Multiple regression techniques

Just as the contingency table can be extended, through the control of
variables, to measure the inter-relationship of more than two
variables, so too can the technique of linear regression. When
investigating the influence of two or more independent variables
upon a single dependent, variable regression coefficients can be
calculated both to measure the *overall* dependence on the explanatory variables, and to compare the contribution made by *each*
variable to the determination of the dependent variable. This
permits the researcher to distinguish statistically between a number
of possible explanatory factors in terms of the effect of each
independent variable on the dependent variable when other
independent variables are being controlled. Such procedures,
however, cannot be entirely unequivocal: as pointed out above,
independent variables will themselves be related and the contribution of one will be more or less effected by its relationship to other

explanatory factors. Multiple regression procedures do, nevertheless, provide statistically reliable indicators of the relative importance of 'competing' explanatory variables.

The statistical procedures for producing multiple regression
figures rely on the production of a series of regression coefficients.
These measure the influence of each explanatory variable upon a
single dependent variable when other explanatory variables are held
constant. In the particular procedure we shall look at (which is
called *stepwise* regression – drawn from the SPSS computer package)
each independent variable, in turn, is correlated with a single
dependent variable: coefficients for each relationship are produced
as are measures of the contribution made by the variables being held
constant. The computer program enters variables one at a time
beginning with the one that explains the greatest amount of variance
in the dependent variable. It then introduces each subsequent
variable in order of its explanatory importance: at each step the
variable that explains the greatest amount of variance *unexplained by
the variables already in the equation* is entered. Before looking at an
example of stepwise regression we should consider the interpretation of the three coefficients which we shall use. In chapter 7 we
encountered two measures used in linear regression – r (the product
moment correlation coefficient), and r^2 (the coefficient of determination). The former represented the strength and direction (positive
or negative) of the relationship; the latter represented the amount of
variation in the dependent variable explained by variation in the
independent variable. Both of these measures are also used in
multiple regression, although they are represented as *Multiple R* and
R^2. In addition, another measure should be noticed here: the *partial
regression coefficient* (represented as B).

The *partial regression coefficient* represents the *expected change in a
dependent variable with a change of one unit in the independent variable
when other independent variables are held constant*. This is similar to the
coefficient of determination but relies on other influencing factors
being controlled, and measures the impact on the dependent
variable of a specified variation in an explanatory variable. In other
words, what we are saying is, if the value of an independent
variable increases by one unit (for example from age 16 to age 17)
what change is produced in the dependent variable? If the value of
the dependent variable decreases with an increase in the independent variable then the B value will be negative; if both variables
increase together, the value will be positive. The more closely
related the variables, the greater the magnitude of the B value.

However, the partial regression coefficient may be quite different in magnitude from other correlation coefficients as the latter will include the influence of other correlated independent variables. You should not be surprised to find fairly small values associated with partial regression coefficients: their usefulness lies particularly in the comparison of the influence of one independent variable with another.

Table 8.3 shows the printout from SPSS of the stepwise regression program. The actual amount of information produced risks bewildering rather than informing the reader but we, as befits novices, can concentrate on the general form of the output and on the three coefficients described above. First, we should note that the variables being used here are not all interval level: the dependent variable 'grade' (ordinal) is being regressed on three explanatory variables, 'age', 'service' and 'gender' (nominal). Regression techniques are best used with interval level variables (as in the scattergram in chapter 7), but one of the virtues of the stepwise procedure is that it will measure the contribution of any form of variable entered. (However, some of the statistical information provided could not be meaningfully used.)

On the eighth line of the printout we find that the variable entered on the first step is 'gender'. In other words, of the three explanatory variables 'gender' explains the greatest amount of variation in grade. The first statistic listed is our correlation coefficient (Multiple R) and its value is 0.32073 – a weak positive correlation. The second statistic is our coefficient of determination (R^2) with a value of 0.10286: this suggests that variation in the variable 'gender' accounts for about 10 per cent of the variation in the variable 'grade'. This seems a very low figure but this may partly be distorted by the fact that 'gender' is a nominal, dichotomous (only two values) variable and therefore the extent of variation is limited.

Underneath the first block of printout we see all three variables listed under headings indicating which variables are included in the equation and which are held constant. For the variable being measured, 'gender', we are given a B value of −0.79740. This requires careful explanation, bearing in mind the interpretation of the partial regression coefficient given above. It indicates that a change of one unit in the variable 'gender' produces a change of about 0.8 units in the dependent variable 'grade'. Moreover, this change is negative – as the value of 'gender' increases, the value of 'grade' decreases. However, we have to remember that 'gender' is

Table 8.3 *Stepwise regression of three explanatory variables on the dependent variable grade*

Variable list number 1. Listwise deletion of missing data.
Equation number 1.
Dependent variable: Grade
Beginning block number 1. Method: Stepwise

Variable(s) entered on step number 1.: Gender

Multiple R	0.32073	Analysis of variance			
R square	0.10286		DF	Sum of squares	Mean square
Adjusted R square	0.10033	Regression	1	56.52555	56.52555
Standard error	1.18009	Residual	354	492.98850	1.39262
		F = 40.58927		Signif F = –.0000	

Variables in the Equation

Variable	B	SE B	Beta	T	SIG T
Gender	–0.79740	0.12516	–0.32073	–6.371	0.0000
(Constant)	2.32065	0.08700		26.675	0.0000

Variables not in the Equation

Variable	Beta In	Partial	Min Toler	T	SIG T
Age	0.11995	0.12561	0.98376	2.379	0.0179
Service	0.18630	0.18898	0.92305	3.616	0.0003

Variables(s) entered on step number 2. Servce

Multiple R	0.36729	Analysis of variance			
R square	0.13490		DF	Sum of squares	Mean square
Adjusted R square	0.13000	Regression	2	74.13127	37.06564
Standard error	1.16047	Residual	353	475.38277	1.34669
		F = 27.52344		Signif F = –.0000	

Variables in the Equation

Variable	B	SE B	Beta	T	SIG T
Gender	–0.66891	0.12811	–0.26905	–5.221	0.0000
Servce	0.03127	0.00865	0.18630	3.616	0.0003
(Constant)	2.04617	0.11438		17.890	0.0000

Variables not in the Equation

Variable	Beta In	Partial	Min Toler	T	SIG T
Age	0.03534	0.03214	0.67125	0.603	0.5467

For block number 1 PIN = 0.050 limits reached.

nominal and an increase, in this sense, represents a change from value 0 (male) to value 1 (female). So the regression coefficient is measuring (what we know from other observations) the negative effect on an employee's grade of being female.

The next variable entered into the equation is 'service'. This has Multiple R = 0.36729 and R^2 = 0.13490, but these figures include the influence of the variable previously entered, 'gender'. In other words, 'service' is the second most important explanatory variable but its additional influence is not very great. This is best represented by the B value for 'service', 0.03127, indicating that the variation explained by 'service' independent of other variables is very small. Finally, we can note that the remaining variable, 'age', is not entered separately into the equation. This is because its influence on the dependent variable is not only less than both the other independent variables, but also falls below the limits set by the program for inclusion. That is, the stepwise computer program will only continue to enter variables if their association with the dependent variable is above a certain pre-specified level.

How, then, can we summarize our multiple regression analysis? Firstly, the stepwise procedure has given us a kind of league table of explanatory variables, listing them in order of importance in their influence on the dependent variable 'grade'. Secondly, it has provided coefficients to measure the contribution made by the influence of each additional variable. Thirdly, it has indicated whether the influence of the independent factors is positive or negative. In every respect this analysis confirms our investigation of these relationships using different techniques in earlier sections. None of the independent variables has a very strong individual influence on grade level, but this is partly because they are all correlated in some degree to each other as well as to the dependent variable (remember the scattergram in chapter 7 showing the relationship of age and service). An employee's gender appears more important in determining grade level than her/his age or length of service and this is mostly attributable to the distribution of women's employment (compare the cross-tabulations in chapter 8.1). Other variables which have not been included here may also be influencing these relationships – level of education, qualifications and training would be factors worth considering.

8.3 Path analysis

There are a number of extensions of multiple regression used in the analysis of multivariate relationships in the social sciences, most of which draw on basically similar principles to those outlined in 8.2 above. It is not within the scope of this book to decribe any large number of these but an example of one, well-known, procedure might help to convey an impression of their general applicability. The example chosen is the procedure known as *path analysis*, a statistical procedure, based upon multiple regression, which has a well-established sociological application and a fairly clear interpretation. Like other regression techniques, path analysis is concerned with measuring the contribution made by a number of independent (though possibly inter-related) variables to the value of a single dependent variable. It derives its name from the initial step in the procedure, which is the construction of a diagram showing the connections or paths between the variables. The diagrams on pp. 139, 140 are examples of this. The arrows indicating the probable connections between variables are regarded as causal paths denoting the direction of determination from independent to dependent variables.

When confronted with a multivariate relationship in which the direction and interconnections between the variables can be partly assumed then the researcher can use path analysis to measure the relative strengths of the relationships between the variables. This then not only clarifies the assumptions made in the path diagram but also enables the researcher to measure the strength of each causal path. The technique was popularized in the social sciences by Duncan[1] in his work on social mobility, and has remained a feature of sociological analysis of mobility patterns.[2] The application in such instances is fairly straightforward. The researcher wishes to explain the position of a particular group of people in terms of a limited number of possible explanatory variables. Obviously, the analysis here is on a relatively high level of generalization: the determination of any one individual's position will involve a multitude of variables, complexly inter-related, but the sociologist must be concerned with only those major influences which effect the class or status position of all individuals. Such variables will include parental occupation, education, gender, and race.

Statistically, path analysis consists of calculating a regression equation for each of the relationships present in a path diagram. As a consequence each 'path' has a regression coefficient (normally referred to as a *path coefficient*) representing the strength of that relationship. As with partial regression coefficients (see section 8.2), the path coefficient represents the proportion of change in a dependent variable attributable to a change in an independent variable, when other variables are held constant. However, as Duncan[3] is at pains to emphasize, the main purpose of path analysis is to provide a clearer *interpretation* of the statistical information. The format of the path diagram permits the researcher to assess whether the assumptions in a hypothetical model are statistically consistent. For this reason it is particularly appropriate in cases where chronologically sequential data are being used. If the time sequence of the variables can be established (e.g. educational attainment must precede occupational status) then a diagram of causal paths can be more confidently constructed. Once such a diagram has been produced then the calculation of path coefficients enables the researcher to evaluate the usefulness of that diagram as an interpretation of the variables which have been measured.

Figure 8.1 shows a path diagram from Duncan's own work on social mobility. At first glance it seems excessively complicated: in fact its interpretation is considerably simpler than one may suspect. The data are from a study of social mobility carried out in Chicago in 1951. Four age groups (or 'cohorts' as they are commonly termed in social mobility study) were studied, and (in this example) three variables measured for each group: occupational status (Y), father's occupational status (X), and respondent's educational attainment (U). Clearly here the dependent variable is Y (occupational status) and what is being measured is the contribution of variables X and U to the value of variable Y. Ideally, the researchers would have studied the same cohort of respondents over different stages of their life but this, of course, raises insuperable obstacles of time and practicality. Instead, making some adjustments to standardize the data as far as possible, Duncan presents the four age groups as if they were four stages in the life cycle of one group of people. Consequently, in the. path diagram, there are four sequential positions for Y: Y_1 (occupational status aged 25–34); Y_2 (occupational status aged 35–44); Y_3 (occupational status aged 45–54); Y_4 (occupational status aged 55–64).

For each of the values of Y a path coefficient has been calculated with the explanatory variables X and U. In addition a path coefficient has been calculated for the two explanatory variables, on the reasonable assumption that father's occupational status will have

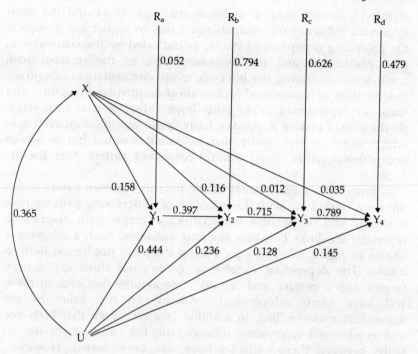

Figure 8.1 *Path diagram of occupational status for four age cohorts*
Y_1 = Occupational Status aged 25–34   X = Father's occupational status
Y_2 = Occupational Status aged 35–44   U = Respondent's educational
                                                                      attainment
Y_3 = Occupational Status aged 45–54
Y_4 = Occupational Status aged 55–64   R = Residual variation
Source: O.D. Duncan, 'Methodological issues in the analysis of social mobility'.

some effect on educational attainment. The other factor is represented as R and this stands for *residual*. The R values for each stage
in the path diagram represent the influence of factors unrelated to
social origins or schooling. What interpretation can then be put on
the coefficients calculated for this diagram? Using Duncan's own
analysis as a starting point, we can make the following observations:
(1) the 'background' factors, father's occupational status and respondent's educational achievement, have an important direct impact
during early stages of a respondent's life cycle (the impact of U on Y
being underpinned by the influence of X on U); (2) after age 35–44
the direct effects of X and U become small or negligible, although
their influence is indirect through the value of initial occupational

status; (3) careers tend to stabilize after age 35–44 and the most important influence on occupational status in higher age groups is the preceding occupational status, as indicated by the sharp rise in path coefficients and the decreasing size of the residual path coefficients; (4) during the life cycle many circumstances essentially independent of background factors affect occupational mobility, and these are represented in the fairly large values of R at each stage; (5) the overall picture suggests a fairly 'loose' stratification system in which status is not rigidly tied to parental status but in which occupational status shows a fairly consistent pattern over the life cycle.

Although the measurement of the data in our own database has not been carried out with the intention of undertaking path analysis it should still be possible to construct a simple path diagram to represent the links between our four variables. Such a diagram is shown in figure 8.2. The logic behind it should not be too hard to follow. The dependent variable is 'grade', our three explanatory factors, 'age', 'gender' and 'service'. We assume that each of these will have some independent influence on the value of the dependent variable. But, in addition, we recognize that both age and gender will have some influence on the value of service, so paths between these variables have also been drawn. However, although we know that gender can't *cause* a change in a respondent's age, there still may be a correlation between the two variables (if, for example, there are very few women above or below a particular age) and so a path has been added between these variables as well. In short, the path diagram attempts to present a visual interpretation of the logical connections between four variables.

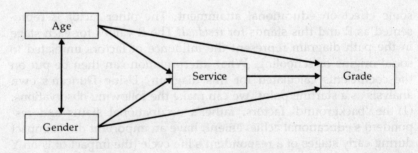

Figure 8.2   *Path diagram of respondent's grade*

Summary

Multivariate analysis consists of statistical techniques which are intended to impose some reliable measurement procedures upon the complexity of relationships encountered in the social sciences. In every instance the techniques are designed to quantify the independent or combined contribution of explanatory variables to the variation in a dependent variable. As will have become obvious the investigation of complex relationships bears similarities to forensic detective work at times – each measurement a new clue to be interpreted and fitted into an overall analysis. This should be part of the reward of statistical analysis, as well as, on occasions, part of its donkey work.

What we have been able to show here is only a guide to the directions followed by researchers using bivariate and multivariate analysis: any real-life project would involve a multitude of similar procedures repeated and extended, often with a very considerable number of variables to consider. No matter how complex the problem, however, the principle remains the same, that it is the ability of the social scientist to construct a useful and realistic explanatory framework in which statistics can be exploited that is crucial: statistical techniques can never do that by themselves.

Further exercises

A Produce contingency tables for the cross-tabulation of 'Gradgp' by 'Agegp' controlling for 'gender'. Interpret the cell values and the associated statistics.

B This would be a good point to look back at the examples given in the book, and the exercises you yourself have undertaken. Can you use the statistical information (1) to give a summary description of the population in terms of each of the four variables; (2) to draw any conclusions about the relationships between the variables; (3) to make comparisons between the parameters of the population and the statistics of samples produced from it?

Notes

1 O.D. Duncan, 'Methodological issues in the analysis of social mobility' in N.J. Smelser and S.M. Lipset (eds), *Social Structure and Mobility – Economic*

Development (Aldine, 1966), pp. 51–77; also in A.P.M. Coxon and C.L. Jones, *Social Mobility* (Harmondsworth, Penguin, 1975) pp. 146–68.

2 A. Heath, *Social Mobility* (Glasgow, Fontana, 1981).

3 Duncan, 'Methodological issues'.

9 Concluding Remarks

At times during the production of this book I have been acutely conscious of the many millions of words already written on the subject of statistics – some of them very wise and valuable words – but have continued in the hope that, nevertheless, this volume might help to meet a particular need. It seems to me inevitable that the use of statistical analysis, computing and graphic illustration will continue to increase in almost every sphere of our lives as workers and consumers. For those in the social science a familiarity with statistical ideas and language will become, if it has not already done so, a prerequisite for virtually all employment. But just to learn statistical techniques, divorced from the context of their production and application, seems as dangerous as to remain ignorant. If this book has an overriding purpose it is to enable the reader to encounter and understand statistics within a meaningful context which incorporates theoretical, conceptual and interpretative concerns.

The most fruitful way of viewing statistical analysis is to regard it not as a separate operation but as an integral part of a sociological evaluation of social phenomena or relationships. Utilizing the procedures described in this book might be compared to carrying out an interview with a survey respondent. Before one can begin the purpose of the interview must be established and the main concerns of the interviewer need to be clarified. The general direction of questioning will be decided upon and perhaps a series of partly or wholly structured questions will be prepared. This is analogous to the construction and clarification of theory, hypotheses and operational concepts in quantitative analysis.

The next stage is the start of the interview itself: straightforward questions at first, to put respondent and interviewer at their ease, perhaps concentrating on general issues or background character- istics of the respondent. Just so, statistically, we begin with an ordering of the data, an overview of its shape and summaries of its characteristics; and the initial description provides direction for more detailed investigation, and a deeper probing into the subject. As the interviewer attempts to 'draw out' his or her subject by an intelligent direction of questioning, so the use of statistics is extended to include more factors and more complex measurement.

Finally, the interviewer may wish to introduce some more speculative questions, to raise issues at the extreme of the interview's main concerns. Similarly, multivariate analysis may provide information which extends investigations and encourages further speculation. At last, in statistics as in the interview, it is the researcher's job to pull everything together, to make sense of information and ideas through the analytic concepts first developed and through the understanding facilitated by the whole process.

In seeing statistical analysis as exploration and analysis, and not just 'number-crunching', its place in social science should seem both more natural and less irksome. For both the student and the researcher there is, after all, a vast potential for the use of quantitative analysis: government data, both national and inter- national, alone provides a huge resource dramatically under-used by social researchers. Social science archives, the work of earlier social researchers, the polls, surveys and investigations undertaken by private companies, all add up to a body of information about our society and lives which we can, and should wish to, explore and understand.

Appendix 1 Database

This database contains 357 cases, each case having a value for each of four variables. A random sample of 89 cases is used from chapter 6 onwards, and the cases included in that sample are indicated with an asterisk. In addition to the four variables each case is identified by a three-digit case number. Some values are coded and a key to these codes is printed at the end.

Case no.	Age	Service	Grade	Gender
*001	16	0	1	0
002	22	0	1	1
003	18	1	1	0
004	17	1	1	1
005	19	2	1	0
006	22	3	5	1
007	51	4	1	0
008	57	4	1	1
009	31	5	4	0
010	32	5	5	1
011	32	7	5	1
012	34	6	5	1
*013	16	0	1	0
014	55	0	1	1
015	17	1	1	0
*016	21	1	1	1
017	55	3	1	0
018	51	4	1	0
019	22	4	1	1

*020	35	5	3	0
021	42	5	4	0
*022	36	7	2	0
023	27	8	1	1
024	40	11	1	0
025	56	20	2	1
026	40	20	2	0
027	31	5	4	0
028	31	7	2	0
*029	55	8	1	1
030	44	11	1	0
031	64	20	2	0
032	17	0	1	0
033	55	0	1	1
034	19	1	1	0
035	21	1	1	1
036	20	2	1	0
037	56	4	1	0
038	51	4	1	1
039	34	5	3	0
*040	32	5	4	0
041	30	7	2	0
042	47	8	1	1
043	58	11	2	0
044	62	20	2	0
*045	32	5	4	0
046	32	7	2	0
047	27	8	1	1
*048	61	11	2	0
049	50	20	2	0
050	18	0	1	0
*051	57	0	1	1
*052	18	0	1	0
053	58	0	1	1
*054	19	1	1	0
055	22	1	1	1
056	25	3	2	0
057	29	4	1	0
058	22	5	1	1
059	33	5	3	0

*060	20	1	1	0
*061	35	1	1	1
062	31	2	2	0
063	59	4	1	0
064	21	5	1	1
065	32	5	3	1
066	18	0	1	0
067	18	0	2	0
068	22	1	1	0
*069	45	1	1	1
*070	55	3	2	0
071	21	4	1	0
*072	21	5	1	1
073	29	5	3	1
074	34	5	4	0
075	30	7	2	0
076	31	8	4	0
077	40	11	1	1
*078	45	20	3	0
079	41	5	4	0
080	31	7	3	0
*081	48	8	4	0
082	50	12	1	0
083	50	21	2	0
*084	41	5	4	0
085	50	7	5	0
086	47	9	1	1
087	40	12	2	0
088	60	21	2	0
089	19	0	1	0
090	18	0	2	0
*091	19	1	1	0
*092	57	1	1	1
093	20	2	3	0
094	21	4	1	0
*095	23	5	1	1
*096	23	5	2	1
097	56	5	5	0
098	25	7	1	1
*099	50	9	1	1

*100	40	12	2	0
*101	59	21	2	0
102	20	0	1	0
103	28	0	2	0
*104	19	1	2	0
105	28	1	1	1
*106	21	3	3	0
*107	22	4	1	0
108	37	5	1	1
109	25	5	2	1
*110	60	5	5	1
111	25	7	1	1
*112	55	9	1	1
113	36	12	3	0
*114	43	22	2	1
115	21	5	5	1
116	47	7	1	1
117	54	9	2	1
*118	60	12	4	0
119	45	22	2	0
120	35	0	1	0
121	31	0	2	1
*122	35	1	2	0
123	28	1	1	1
124	21	2	3	0
125	24	4	1	0
126	38	5	1	1
*127	22	5	2	1
128	42	0	1	0
129	27	0	3	0
*130	37	1	2	0
131	57	1	1	1
132	21	2	3	0
*133	26	4	1	0
134	58	5	1	1
135	22	5	2	1
136	24	5	5	1
*137	25	7	1	1
138	29	9	2	1
139	42	12	4	0

140	45	23	2	0
*141	22	5	5	1
142	26	7	1	1
*143	50	9	5	1
144	28	13	1	1
145	55	23	2	0
146	22	5	5	1
147	26	7	1	1
148	35	9	4	0
149	61	13	2	0
150	50	24	2	0
151	45	0	1	0
152	31	0	4	0
153	50	1	4	0
*154	20	1	2	1
155	22	2	3	0
156	26	4	1	0
157	27	5	1	1
158	21	5	2	1
159	21	5	5	1
160	36	7	1	1
161	35	9	4	0
162	43	13	4	0
163	47	24	2	0
*164	22	6	1	0
165	55	7	1	1
*166	41	9	4	0
167	43	13	4	0
168	55	24	3	0
169	16	0	1	1
170	32	0	4	0
171	50	1	4	0
172	20	1	3	1
173	31	3	4	0
*174	51	4	1	0
175	47	5	1	1
176	16	0	1	1
177	16	0	1	1
*178	32	0	4	0
179	22	6	1	0

180	27	7	1	1
181	50	9	4	0
182	33	14	2	0
*183	50	24	2	0
*184	60	1	4	0
185	30	1	3	1
*186	32	2	4	0
187	27	4	1	0
188	47	5	1	1
189	24	4	1	1
190	33	0	4	0
191	60	1	4	0
192	30	1	3	1
193	33	3	4	0
194	52	4	1	0
195	52	5	1	1
*196	58	4	1	1
197	17	0	1	1
198	18	1	1	1
199	55	1	5	1
200	55	2	5	0
201	37	4	1	0
202	40	5	1	1
203	22	4	1	1
204	22	4	1	1
205	56	5	1	1
206	22	4	1	1
207	35	2	1	1
*208	17	1	1	1
209	18	0	1	1
210	18	0	1	1
211	20	1	1	1
212	20	2	1	1
213	21	4	1	1
*214	48	5	1	1
215	22	4	1	1
216	25	6	1	0
217	49	7	1	1
*218	41	10	1	0
*219	40	14	3	0

*220	53	24	2	0
221	25	6	1	0
222	18	0	1	1
223	20	1	1	1
224	20	2	1	1
*225	21	4	1	1
226	22	5	2	0
227	58	4	1	1
228	18	0	1	1
229	21	1	1	1
230	20	2	1	1
*231	22	4	1	1
232	22	5	2	0
233	57	4	1	1
234	29	7	1	1
235	46	10	1	0
236	48	14	4	0
237	52	26	2	0
238	36	6	1	0
239	29	7	1	1
240	30	10	1	0
241	46	14	1	1
242	43	27	4	0
*243	19	0	1	1
244	22	1	1	1
245	30	2	1	1
246	24	4	1	1
247	30	5	2	0
248	55	4	1	1
249	19	0	1	1
250	22	1	1	1
251	20	3	1	1
252	30	4	1	1
253	30	5	2	0
*254	55	4	1	1
255	20	0	1	1
256	24	1	1	1
257	20	3	1	1
*258	45	4	1	1
259	34	5	2	0

*260	28	4	1	1
261	48	6	1	0
262	39	7	1	1
*263	62	10	1	0
264	56	14	2	1
265	56	27	3	0
*266	38	6	1	0
267	39	7	1	1
268	33	10	2	0
269	59	14	2	1
*270	50	28	4	0
271	29	6	2	0
272	48	7	1	1
*273	41	10	2	0
274	57	13	2	1
*275	60	29	3	0
276	20	0	1	1
277	26	1	1	1
278	21	3	1	1
*279	50	4	1	1
280	24	5	2	0
*281	35	4	1	1
282	20	0	1	1
283	26	1	1	1
284	45	3	1	1
285	28	4	1	1
286	31	5	2	0
287	35	4	1	1
288	30	6	2	0
*289	53	7	1	1
*290	56	10	2	0
291	42	15	2	0
292	64	31	4	0
293	20	0	1	1
*294	22	0	1	1
*295	35	1	1	1
*296	46	3	1	1
297	46	4	1	1
298	37	5	2	0
299	56	4	1	1

*300	32	6	2	0
*301	29	6	3	0
302	56	8	1	0
303	32	10	2	0
304	50	15	2	0
305	59	31	3	0
*306	30	6	1	1
*307	34	8	2	0
308	32	10	4	0
*309	50	16	2	0
310	50	34	4	0
311	47	8	2	0
312	44	10	4	0
313	44	16	4	0
314	54	34	4	0
*315	38	1	1	1
*316	48	3	1	1
317	46	4	1	1
318	38	5	2	0
319	56	4	1	1
320	23	0	1	1
*321	49	0	1	1
322	42	1	1	1
*323	20	2	2	1
324	56	4	1	1
325	41	5	2	0
326	59	4	1	0
327	49	1	1	1
328	36	2	3	1
329	56	4	1	1
330	29	6	1	1
331	42	6	1	1
*332	32	8	2	0
*333	61	10	4	0
*334	53	17	2	0
335	54	35	4	0
336	61	38	4	0
337	43	7	1	0
338	50	7	1	0
339	34	8	2	0

340	45	8	2	0
*341	59	39	2	1
*342	59	18	2	1
343	44	11	4	0
344	45	8	3	0
345	57	8	1	1
346	36	10	1	1
347	61	39	4	0
348	43	10	1	1
*349	54	38	2	1
350	22	1	5	1
351	54	19	4	0
352	54	19	4	0
*353	54	17	2	0
354	22	3	5	1
355	55	18	2	0
356	43	11	1	0
*357	44	19	4	0

Coding of variables

Variables 'age' and 'service' not been coded. Both are measured in *completed* years, hence employees with less than one whole year's service are given the score zero.

Variables 'grade' and 'gender' are both coded as shown below.

Grade:

All clerical grades	1
Administrative, technical and professional (APT)	2
Senior officer	3
Principal officer	4
Other grades (mainly secretarial)	5

Gender:

Male	0
Female	1

Appendix 2
A glossary of common terms

This glossary is arranged not alphabetically but sequentially, so that related definitions appear together, according to the chapter in which they are first encountered in the main text.

Chapter 3

Case The basic unit of analysis. Also called an *observation*.

Population All the cases with which we are concerned in a particular study. Also called a *universe*.

Sample A number of cases selected from the population, normally selected randomly to represent the population as a whole.

Variable An attribute of a population which varies. Each variable will have a number of possible values but each case will have one, and only one, value for each variable.

Value The category, rank position or score taken by each case for each variable.

Coding The allocation of *numerical* codes for each value of a variable, in order to permit computerized analysis.

Levels of measurement Three levels of classification of variables:
Nominal: classification of values into useful categories or codes. Numerical codes are just like names and imply no particular order or relationship between the values.

Ordinal: Ordering of categories on a single scale. Implies a ranking but does not indicate the distance between each category.

Interval: Ordering of categories and measurement of distance between them. Implies the use of a common unit of measurement. Codes can be real numbers and thus be manipulated mathematically. *Ratio* level is a variable at interval level but with an identifiable zero.

Types of variable   Distinction between variables on the basis of the type of their values.

Discrete: Values cannot be broken down any further; separate categories – not all values possible.

Continuous: All values are theoretically possible – an unbroken continuum. Actual categories depend on the accuracy of measurement used.

Aggregated: (or *grouped*) values can be used to simplify analysis by putting a number of values together in a single category. Aggregated values should not be treated as basic units: doing this is termed the *ecological fallacy*.

Chapter 4

Descriptive statistics   Techniques used to measure, order and summarize data in numerical and pictorial form.

Frequency distribution   The distribution of cases between the possible values for each variable.

Relative frequency   The number of cases which occur for each value of any one variable. Represented either as a number of cases or a *percentage* of the total number of cases.

Cumulative frequency   Each relative frequency added to the previous one. Demonstrates the percentage of cases falling above or below each value (but is consequently not usable with nominal level variables).

Proportion   A number of cases represented as a fraction of the total number of cases (e.g. the proportion of cases in one particular category).

Percentage   A proportion, when the total number of cases is treated as 100.

Ratio The number of cases taking one value compared to the total number of cases, or to the number of cases taking all, or some, of the other possible values. Commonly represented in terms of the number of cases taking one value for each *one* case taking another value.

Histogram Visual representation of the number of cases taking each value, either as a line of asterisks (e.g. in SPSS printout), or as continuous lines, or as blocks or bars on two axes.

Bar chart A histogram using equal intervals (i.e. the width of each bar is the same), thus making the area of the bar proportional to the number of cases it represents. *Compound* or *component* bar charts subdivide each bar to show the distribution of another related variable.

Frequency polygon A line formed by joining the mid-points of each bar on a bar chart. A graphic representation of distribution, but it cannot be treated as a graph (i.e. it is *not* to be read as a continuous line).

Chapter 5

Mean The values of all the cases added together and divided by the number of cases. Appropriate for interval variables only.

Median The value of the middle case in a series from the lowest to the highest value. Appropriate for ordinal and interval variables.

Mode The most frequently occurring value. Appropriate for any level of measurement.

Range The difference between the highest and the lowest occurring values in a distribution.

Percentiles The division of a distribution into equal parts. *Quartiles* divide the distribution into 4: *deciles* into 10; *percentiles* into 100. Appropriate for ordinal and interval level variables.

Standard deviation A measure of the deviation or difference, of the values from the mean value. Expresses the *variability* of the values from the mean value. Expresses the *variability* of the distribution.

Coefficient of variation An expression of the relative homogeneity of a distribution, calculated by dividing the standard deviation by the mean. Enables us to compare samples with means and standard deviations of a different magnitude.

Distribution curves   Smooth curves representing frequency distributions, where the area under the curve represents the total number of cases; sometimes possessing particular mathematical properties: notably, the *normal curve*.

Normal curve   A bell-shaped curve, symmetrical about its mean, which represents a (theoretical) distribution in which mean, median and modal values are identical.

Bimodal curve   A curve representing a distribution with two modal values or, in practice, two fairly similar peaks in the distribution of cases.

Peakedness   The extent to which a distribution curve is peaked or flat. The smaller the standard deviation relative to the mean, the more peaked the curve (and *vice versa*).

Skewness   The extent to which a distribution curve is inclined towards extreme values, making the mean either lower than the median (a *negatively* skewed curve) or higher than the median (a *positively* skewed curve).

Chapter 6

Inductive statistics   Techniques used to study the characteristics of a population on the basis of studying known facts about a sample drawn from that population. Also referred to as *inferential* statistics.

Population parameter   A fixed but (normally) unknown value referring to the population.

Sample statistic   A value which is known but which may vary from sample to sample.

Sampling error   The difference between the sample statistic and the population parameter. Sampling error is due to *random sampling error* (the unavoidable difference in the constitution of a sample and the constitution of the population from which it was drawn), and *bias* (the distortion of a sample due to the disproportionate influence of one particular factor).

Random sample A sample taken in such a way that every member of the population has an equal chance of selection as a member of the sample. Normally based on a table of *random numbers*.

Sampling frame The list of cases from which the sample is drawn. The construction of the sampling frame is a common source of *bias*.

Standard error of the mean The standard deviation of a sampling distribution. Used to estimate the population mean from the sample mean.

Confidence level The level of confidence or certainty with which we can estimate the population mean from the sample mean (e.g. 95 per cent confidence means that our estimation will be correct 19 times out of 20 or, conversely, that we risk being wrong one time out of 20).

Confidence interval The range of values within which our population mean will lie. The size of the confidence interval will depend on the confidence level selected: the higher the confidence level, the greater the confidence interval.

Test of significance Used to test whether a statistical outcome is due solely to chance (e.g. whether the difference between a predicted population mean and a sample mean is due to chance alone or due to a mistaken prediction). A difference not due to chance alone is said to be *statistically significant*.

Level of significance Differences can be statistically significant at different levels. We select a level of significance just as we select a level of confidence in the estimation of population parameters. The appropriate level of significance depends on the importance of the hypothesis being tested and on how confident we want to be that our conclusion is correct.

Hypothesis A statement, or an assumption about a specified situation or outcome which can be tested on the basis of known facts.

Null hypothesis A hypothesis stated in such a way that enables it to be rejected.

Student's 't' A test of significance designed to test hypotheses concerning population and/or sample means.

Chapter 7

Multivariate analysis   Techniques used to investigate the relationship between two (bivariate) or more (multivariate) variables in a sample.

Contingency table   A table showing the relation of two variables in raw frequencies and percentages. Each value of each variable constitutes a *row* or a *column* of the table which is designated by its size (e.g. 'a four (rows) by two (columns) table'). The table consists of a number of *cells*, the smallest table having four cells (two by two).

Chi-square   A common test of significance used with contingency tables, and based on the statistical difference between *observed* and *expected frequencies*. Appropriate for nominal level variables and higher, it demonstrates only the *existence* of a relationship.

Observed frequencies   The frequencies which actually occur in a distribution.

Expected frequencies   The frequencies which would occur *were there no relationship between the variables*.

Measure of association   A measure used in conjunction with significance tests to assess the *strength* of a relationship between variables. Expressed as a value between 0 and 1 (for nominal variables) or between −1 and +1 (for ordinal and interval variables).

Correlation coefficient   Measures of association used with ordinal and interval level variables.

Perfect association   A situation in which change in one variable produces an equal change in a related variable, either *positive* (variable B increases as variable A increases) or *negative* (variable B decreases as variable A increases). The value of one variable can be predicted exactly from the value of the other variable.

Rank order correlation   A test of the relationship between *ordinal* level variables.

Spearman's 'r'   A coefficient of rank order correlation. The value of the coefficient indicates the strength of the relationship, ranging from −1 (perfect negative) through 0 (no relation) to +1 (perfect positive).

Kendall's tau Another measure of association used for ordinal level variables and interpreted in the same way as Spearman's r.

Pearson's 'r' Also called the *product-moment correlation coefficient*. A measure of association used with interval level variables and measured on a scale −1 to +1.

Scattergram Representation on graph axes of bivariate data in which each point represents a pair of values, one for the independent, one for the dependent variable.

Line of 'best fit' A line drawn through the points on a scattergram to produce a linear representation of the relationship between the two variables being measured. Can be calculated using the *method of least squares*. Also referred to as a *regression line*.

Chapter 8

Controlled variable A variable the value of which is held constant in the presence of other variables.

Coefficient of determination (r^2) A coefficient representing the amount of variation in a dependent variable explained by variation in a given independent variable.

Partial regression coefficient (B) A coefficient representing the expected change in a dependent variable with a change of one unit in an independent variable (all others held constant).

Path diagram A technique designed to aid interpretation of multivariate relationships by the construction of a diagram of causal 'paths' and the calculation of a *path coefficient* for each path between variables.

Appendix 3　A guide to simple algebraic notation

Most statistical textbooks use a considerable amount of algebraic notation to represent the mathematical formulae upon which statistical procedures depend. The decision to avoid such notation in this book was taken in the light of our experience of students' difficulty with comprehending and utilizing algebra. Not only does it present an additional learning task for those without recent mathematical experience, but it may also constitute an obstacle to the understanding of the statistical procedures themselves. Moreover, in a world in which virtually all statistical analysis is undertaken by computer, the traditional requirement for students to work laboriously through examples using mathematical formulae seems at best superfluous and, at worst, alienating.

Nevertheless, some simple formulae and algebraic symbols are used in this book as the student will encounter these both in the literature and in computer programs. Definitions of the most common are given below. (N.B. Conventionally, Greek letters are used to represent characteristics of a population (parameters).)

Algebraic notation

Median	= Md
Mean	= $\bar{X}$ (sample)
	μ (population)
Sum of values	= Σ
Number of cases	= n or N
Frequency	= f or F
Standard deviation	= s (sample)
	= σ (population)

Greater than	$= >$
Less than	$= <$
Greater than or equal to	$= \geq$
Chi-square	$= \chi^2$
Spearman's rank order correlation coefficient	$= p(rho)$
Coefficient of determination	$= r^2$
Pearson's p-m coefficient	$= r$
Square	$= x^2$
Square root	$= \sqrt{}$
Probability (in tests of significance)	$= P$ (e.g. $P > 0.005$)

Appendix 4 Software for statistical analysis

The overwhelming majority of statistical calculations carried out in contemporary sociology are done using the speed, accuracy and capacity of computers. Until fairly recently most of this was done by *batch processing* on *mainframe* computers: that is, a 'batch' of data and programmed instructions would be entered into the large, central computer of the institution responsible for the research by means of *punched cards*, *magnetic tape* or *disk*. The results of the processing would be available as printed output (*printout*) within a period of time determined by the overall demands on the computer's capacity. This system changed with the introduction of *decentralized* or *distributed* processing whereby computer users could enter data directly to the computer by means of their own computer *terminal*. Files of data stored on the computer could be modified and new instructions initiated immediately: ideally, this would be done *interactively*, so that the modifications could be seen on the user's *visual display unit* without any significant intervening delay.

An even greater change came with the advent of *mini-* or *micro-computers*: small computers equipped with the facilities of a mainframe but on a much reduced scale and cost. Data entry, alteration and analysis was now possible with complete autonomy as the individual sociologist or department could possess their own *hardware* (the computer machinery itself) and *software* (the *programs* of instructions for performing jobs on the computer).

The limitations on the use of microcomputers in sociological research are twofold: size and software. The smaller capacity of the micro-computer means that very large bodies of data cannot be entered or retained on these machines. Similarly, micros cannot handle very complex statistical programs which require the resources of a much larger computer. Consequently mainframes are still very much part of statistical life for social scientists, although the use of micros will continue to expand rapidly as their capacities and sophistication are extended. Also increasing rapidly is the range of software available for statistical analysis on micro-computers and this now effectively parallels the software developed for their larger predecessors. However, whereas statistical software on mainframes has been dominated by a small number of well known packages of programs, the hectic pace of microcomputer development has brought a large number of similar programs onto the market in a short space of time. To make things more confusing many of these programs have been developed for use on one, and only one, make of computer and are not *compatible* with other manufacturers' products.

It would be impossible and, given the pace of innovation, probably fruitless to attempt a survey of the software available and would still give no indication of the quality or applicability of the competing programs. It does seem worthwhile, nevertheless, to mention at least some of the programs and *packages* of programs available for the most popular microcomputers in the hope that it will provide an initial guide for the student, teacher or researcher who is in the position of selecting a micro and/or software for the primary purpose of statistical analysis. Choosing and using computers can be as frustrating as it can be rewarding but undoubtedly repays the time and effort put into it. Reviews of software can regularly be found in the many computer-oriented magazines as well as, more occasionally, in statistical journals. The table on p. 167 lists a number of microcomputers and some of the software available for them. Where possible I have indicated the range of statistical procedures offered by the software. There are also a number of *data packages* available which contain statistical material for the student to analyse both as an exercise in computer learning and as a substantive exercise in social science. Details of these are available from software manufacturers. It would be impossible to over-emphasize the utility to the contemporary social scientist of acquiring some familiarity with the use of computers. Even for the student whose formal sociology ends with the acquisition of a degree the ability to feel at home with microcomputers will be an asset which is unlikely to go unused in later life.

Statistical analysis on mainframe computers has long been associated with one package of programs – SPSS (Statistical Package for the Social Sciences) – which provides a very substantial range of the procedures required not just by social scientists but by statisticians in related fields as well. Indeed the instruction manual for SPSS (Nie et al., *Statistical Package for the Social Sciences*, 1975) is, in itself, a useful introductory guide to statistical procedures and a valuable reference book on what techniques are available to the social scientist. The main SPSS package has gone into a number of versions (most recently SPSSX) and a scaled-down version (SPSSPC) has also been produced, specifically designed for the version of the IBM Personal Computer with a fairly large (320k) memory. However, other similar programs have been developed and in recent years the package MINITAB has emerged as a serious alternative to SPSS. This, like SPSS, was initially available as a complete package of statistical procedures for use on mainframe computers. However, it too has been converted for use on micro-computers, although again it is too large a system for very small machines to cope with. The choice for the social scientist wishing to utilize statistical packages will probably be severely limited by available resources and, possibly, constrained by the necessity of using hardware already established in his or her institution or company. In which case choices between competing packages will be influenced first by *compatibility* ('does this package operate on my computer?'), second by cost ('which of these are within my budget?') and finally by the user's objectives ('what do I want from this package?'). The third question requires considerable thought: a package offering an impressive range of complex programs may not be the most suitable if it is to be used as a vehicle for teaching computer analysis. The best guide here is other people's experience: whether you're buying for yourself, for a research project or unit, or for a teaching institution, talk first to as many people as possible who have used different systems themselves.

The following list draws heavily on the listing compiled by Hugh Neffendorf of Systematic (112 Strand, London WC2R 0AA), who can provide more detailed and updated information. Inclusion or exclusion from the list provided here does not imply recommend-ation or otherwise.

Software for statistical analysis on microcomputer

Software package	Software capabilities	Software supplier	Computer compatibility
SPSSPC	Unlimited number of cases for up to 150 variables. Most procedures found on full scale SPSSX		IBM PC with 320k memory
SPSS/Pro	Similar to above but for DEC Professional 350		
Minitab	Scaled-down version of mainframe package		IBM PC with 256k memory DEC Pro.350 Apollo Wicat Hewlett-Packard 200 Fortune Wang Rainbow
Abstat	Data manipulation, editing, histograms, random numbers, contingency tables, chi-square, regression etc.	Anderson-Bell, 2916 South Stuart St, Denver, Colorado 80236	CP/M operating systems with 56k memory; also IBM PC with 1284k memory
Chart	Data series manipulation with sophisticated range of charts and diagrams	Microsoft Ltd, Piper House, Hatch Lane Windsor, SL4 3QJ	Macintosh
Conduit	Computer-based learning materials for statistics teaching	Conduit, 100 Lindquist Centre, Univ. of Iowa, PO Box 388, Iowa City, IA 52244	Apple
Daisy Professional	All descriptive statistics, correlation, histograms, scatter plots, etc.	Rainbow Computing Inc, 8811 Amigo Ave., Northridge, CA	Apple II

continued

Software package	Software capabilities	Software supplier	Computer compatibility
DATA-X	Data editing, non-parametric, ANOVA, regression, descriptive, manipulation	Patrick Royston, 85 Canfield Gardens, London, NW6 3EA	PET
Graph/Stats II	Easy-to-use graphics package including flow, pie and line charts, three-dimensional charts	R.S. Ball, Freepost, Birkenhead, Merseyside, L42 2AB	BBC Micro
INTER-STAT	Descriptive, distributions, tests, chi-square, regression, plots	Great Northern Computer Services (0423) 501131	Apple II
Modistat	Graphics and statistics program with database management, histograms, line charts, scatter plots etc.	Modicom	IBM PC, XT Compaq Other PCDOS systems with 256k memory
Number Cruncher Stat System	Data management, contingency tables, correlation, regression etc.	NLSS, 865 East 400 North, Kaysville, Utah 84037	Macintosh 128k memory
Statfast	Descriptive statistics, correlation, t-tests, regression etc.	Statsoft, 2831 East 10th Street, Suite 3, Tulso, Oklahoma 74104	Macintosh 128k memory
Statflow	Data management, simple graphics, for charts, scattergrams, correlation, regression etc.	Great Northern Computer Services (0423) 501131	IBM PC, XT

Software package	Software capabilities	Software supplier	Computer compatibility
STATPAK	File management, probability, descriptive, regression, non-parametric, distributions, tests, chi-square, ANOVA, plots, random numbers	Northwest Analytical Inc., PO Box 14430, Portland, Oregon 97214	CP/M
Statpro	Full range of descriptive statistics, correlation etc.; data management and graphical analysis	Wadsworth Prod-Software	IBM PC
Statsease	Database manage-descriptive statistics, correlation and regression		Apple II with 48k memory
Statworks	Descriptive and multivariate statistics, graphics including three-dimensional charts	Wadsworth Prod-Software	IBM PC

Appendix 5 Statistical Tables

Table A5.1 *Random numbers*

Line/Col.	1	2	3	4	5	6	7	8	9	10	11	12	13	14
1	10480	15011	01536	02011	81647	91646	69179	14194	62590	36207	20969	99570	91291	90700
2	22368	46573	25595	85393	30995	89198	27982	53402	93965	34095	52666	19174	39615	99505
3	24130	48360	22527	97265	76393	64809	15179	24830	49340	32081	30680	19655	63348	58629
4	42167	93093	06243	61680	07856	16376	39440	53537	71341	57004	00849	74917	97758	16379
5	37570	39975	81837	16656	06121	91782	60468	81305	49684	60672	14110	06927	01263	54613
6	77921	06907	11008	42751	27756	53498	18602	70659	90655	15053	21916	81825	44394	42800
7	99562	72905	56420	69994	98872	31016	71194	18738	44013	48840	63213	21069	10634	12952
8	96301	91977	05463	07972	18876	20922	94595	56869	69014	60045	18425	84903	42508	32307
9	89579	14342	63661	10281	17453	18103	57740	84378	25331	12566	58678	44947	05585	56941
10	85475	36857	53342	53988	53060	59533	38867	62300	08158	17983	16439	11458	18593	64952

11	28918	69578	88231	33276	70997	79936	56865	05859	90106	31595	01547	85590	91610	78188
12	63553	40961	48235	03427	49626	69445	18663	72695	52180	20847	12234	90511	33703	90322
13	09429	93969	52636	92737	88974	33488	36320	17617	30015	08272	84115	27156	30613	74952
14	10365	61129	87529	85689	48237	52267	67689	93394	01511	26358	85104	20285	29975	89868
15	07119	97336	71048	08178	77233	13916	47564	81056	97735	85977	29372	74461	28551	90707
16	51085	12765	51821	51259	77452	16308	60756	92144	49442	53900	70960	63990	75601	40719
17	02368	21382	52404	60268	89368	19885	55322	44819	01188	65255	64835	44919	05944	55157
18	01011	54092	33362	94904	31273	04146	18594	29852	71585	85030	51132	01915	92747	64951
19	52162	53916	46369	58586	23216	14513	83149	98736	23495	64350	94738	17752	35156	35749
20	07056	97628	33787	09998	42698	06691	76988	13602	51851	46104	88916	19509	25625	58104
21	48663	91245	85828	14346	09172	30168	90229	04734	59193	22178	30421	61666	99904	32812
22	54164	58492	22421	74103	47070	25306	76468	26384	58151	06646	21524	15227	96909	44592
23	32639	32363	05597	24200	13363	38005	94342	28728	35806	06912	17012	64161	18296	22851
24	29334	27001	87637	87308	58731	00256	45834	15398	46557	41135	10367	07684	36188	18510
25	02488	33062	28834	07351	19731	92420	60952	61280	50001	67658	32586	86679	50720	94953

Source: L. Ott, R.F. Larson and W. Mendenhall, *Statistics: A Tool for the Social Sciences* (3rd edn, Massachusetts, Duxbury Press, 1983)

Table A5.2 *Distribution of t*

df	| Level of significance for one-tailed test					
	.10	.05	.025	.01	.005	.0005
	| Level of significance for two-tailed test					
	.20	.10	.05	.02	.01	.001
1	3.078	6.314	12.706	31.821	63.657	636.619
2	1.886	2.920	4.303	6.965	9.925	31.598
3	1.638	2.353	3.182	4.541	5.841	12.941
4	1.533	2.132	2.776	3.747	4.604	8.610
5	1.476	2.015	2.571	3.365	4.032	6.859
6	1.440	1.943	2.447	3.143	3.707	5.959
7	1.415	1.895	2.365	2.998	3.499	5.405
8	1.397	1.860	2.306	2.896	3.355	5.041
9	1.383	1.833	2.262	2.821	3.250	4.781
10	1.372	1.812	2.228	2.764	3.169	4.587
11	1.363	1.796	2.201	2.718	3.106	4.497
12	1.356	1.782	2.179	2.681	3.055	4.318
13	1.350	1.771	2.160	2.650	3.012	4.221
14	1.345	1.761	2.145	2.624	2.977	4.140
15	1.341	1.753	2.131	2.602	2.947	4.073
16	1.337	1.746	2.120	2.583	2.921	4.015
17	1.333	1.740	2.110	2.567	2.898	3.965
18	1.330	1.734	2.101	2.552	2.878	3.922
19	1.328	1.729	2.093	2.539	2.861	3.883
20	1.325	1.725	2.086	2.528	2.845	3.850
21	1.323	1.721	2.080	2.518	2.831	3.819
22	1.321	1.717	2.074	2.508	2.819	3.792
23	1.319	1.714	2.069	2.500	2.807	3.767
24	1.318	1.711	2.064	2.492	2.797	3.745
25	1.316	1.708	2.060	2.485	2.787	3.725
26	1.315	1.706	2.056	2.479	2.779	3.707
27	1.314	1.703	2.052	2.473	2.771	3.690
28	1.313	1.701	2.048	2.467	2.763	3.674
29	1.311	1.699	2.045	2.462	2.756	3.659
30	1.310	1.697	2.042	2.457	2.750	3.646

Table A5.2   *continued*

df	Level of significance for one-tailed test					
	.10	.05	.025	.01	.005	.0005
	Level of significance for two-tailed test					
	.20	.10	.05	.02	.01	.001
40	1.303	1.684	2.021	2.423	2.704	3.551
60	1.296	1.671	2.000	2.390	2.660	3.460
120	1.289	1.658	1.980	2.358	2.617	3.373
∞	1.282	1.645	1.960	2.326	2.576	3.291

Source: H.M. Blalock, *Social Statistics* (2nd edn, McGraw-Hill, 1972)

Table A5.3 Distribution of χ^2

df	.99	.98	.95	.90	.80	.70	.50	.30	.20	.10	.05	.02	.01	.001
							Probability							
1	.0²157	.0³028	.00393	.0158	.0042	.148	.455	1.074	1.642	2.706	3.841	5.412	6.635	10.827
2	.0201	.0401	.103	.211	.446	.713	1.386	2.408	3.219	4.605	5.991	7.824	9.210	13.815
3	.115	.185	.352	.584	1.005	1.424	2.366	3.665	4.642	6.251	7.815	9.837	11.341	16.268
4	.297	.429	.711	1.064	1.049	2.195	3.357	4.878	5.989	7.779	9.488	11.668	13.277	18.465
5	.554	.752	1.145	1.610	2.343	3.000	4.351	6.064	7.289	9.236	11.070	13.388	15.086	20.517
6	872	1.134	1.635	2.204	3.070	3.828	5.348	7.231	8.558	10.645	12.592	15.033	16.812	22.457
7	1.239	1.564	2.167	2.833	3.822	4.071	6.346	8.383	9.803	12.017	14.067	16.622	18.475	24.322
8	1.646	2.032	2.733	3.400	4.594	5.527	7.344	9.524	11.030	13.362	15.507	18.168	20.090	26.125
9	2.088	2.532	3.325	4.168	5.380	6.393	8.343	10.656	12.242	14.684	16.910	19.679	21.666	27.877
10	2.558	3.059	3.940	4.865	6.179	7.267	9.342	11.781	13.442	15.987	18.307	21.161	23.209	29.588
11	3.053	3.609	4.575	5.578	6.989	8.148	10.341	12.899	14.631	17.275	19.675	22.618	24.725	31.264
12	3.571	4.178	5.226	6.304	7.807	9.034	11.340	14.011	15.812	18.549	21.026	24.054	26.217	32.909
13	4.107	4.765	5.892	7.042	8.634	9.926	12.340	15.119	16.985	19.812	22.362	25.472	27.688	34.528
14	4.668	5.368	6.571	7.790	9.467	10.821	13.339	16.222	18.151	21.064	23.085	26.873	29.141	36.123
15	5.229	5.985	7.261	8.347	10.307	11.721	14.339	17.322	19.311	22.307	24.996	28.250	30.578	37.097

df														
16	5.812	6.014	7.062	9.312	11.152	12.624	15.338	18.418	20.405	23.542	26.296	29.633	32.000	39.252
17	6.408	7.255	8.672	10.085	12.002	13.531	16.338	19.511	21.615	24.769	27.587	30.995	33.409	40.790
18	7.015	7.996	9.390	10.865	12.857	14.440	17.338	20.601	22.760	25.989	28.869	32.346	34.805	42.312
19	7.633	8.567	10.117	11.651	13.716	15.352	18.338	21.689	23.900	27.204	30.114	33.687	36.191	43.820
20	8.200	9.237	10.851	12.448	14.578	16.266	19.337	22.775	25.038	28.412	31.410	35.020	37.566	45.315
21	8.897	9.915	11.591	13.240	15.445	17.182	20.337	23.858	26.171	29.615	32.671	36.343	38.932	46.797
22	9.542	10.600	12.338	14.041	16.314	18.101	21.337	24.939	27.301	30.813	33.924	37.659	40.289	48.268
23	10.196	11.203	13.091	14.848	17.187	19.021	22.337	26.018	28.429	32.007	35.172	36.908	41.638	49.728
24	10.856	11.992	13.843	15.659	18.063	19.943	23.337	27.096	29.553	33.196	36.415	40.270	42.980	51.179
25	11.524	12.697	14.611	16.473	18.940	20.867	24.337	28.172	30.675	34.382	37.652	41.565	44.314	52.620
26	12.198	13.409	15.379	17.292	19.820	21.792	25.336	29.246	31.795	35.566	38.885	42.856	45.642	54.052
27	12.879	14.125	16.151	18.114	20.703	22.719	26.336	30.319	32.912	36.741	40.113	44.140	46.963	55.476
28	13.565	14.847	16.928	18.939	21.588	23.647	27.336	31.391	34.027	37.916	41.337	45.419	48.278	56.893
29	14.256	15.574	17.768	19.768	22.475	24.577	28.336	32.461	35.139	39.087	42.557	46.603	49.588	58.302
30	14.938	16.306	18.493	20.599	23.364	25.503	29.336	33.530	36.250	40.256	43.773	47.962	50.892	59.703

Source: H.M. Blalock, *Social Statistics* (2nd edn, New York, McGraw-Hill, 1972)

$$c^2 \quad V = \phi = \sqrt{\frac{x^2}{N}} \quad V = \sqrt{\frac{x^2}{N(k-1)}}$$

Bibliography

The following sources are cited in the text. Those marked with an asterisk are recommended as sources of further reading and practice examples.

Bain, G.S. and Price, R., 'Union growth: dimensions, determinants, and destiny', in G.S. Bain (ed), *Industrial Relations in Britain* (Oxford, Basil Blackwell, 1983).

Barnes, J.A., *Who Should Know What?* (Harmondsworth, Penguin, 1979).

Bell, C. and Newby, H. (eds), *Doing Sociological Research* (London, Allen and Unwin, 1977).

Blalock, H.M., *An Introduction to Social Research* (New Jersey, Prentice-Hall Inc., 1970).

*Blalock, H.M., *Social Statistics*, (2nd edn, New York, McGraw-Hill, 1972).

Booth, C., *Life and Labour of the People of London* (9 vols, London, Macmillan, 1892–97).

Brown, B., 'Exactly what we wanted', in M. Barker, *The Video Nasties* (London, Pluto Press, 1984).

Brown, B., 'Nasty report that left out the factual niceties', *The Guardian*, 24 September 1984.

Bulmer, M., *Sociological Research Methods. An Introduction* (London, Macmillan, 1977).

Cicourel, A., *Method and Measurement* (New York, The Free Press, 1964).

Duncan, O.D., 'Methodlogical issues in the analysis of social mobility' in N.J. Smelser and S.M. Lipset (eds), *Social Structure and Mobility in Economic Development* (Aldine, 1966), pp. 51–97; also in A.P.M. Coxon and C.L. Jones, *Social Mobility* (Harmondsworth, Penguin, 1975), pp. 146–68.

Durkheim, E., *Suicide*, trans. J.A. Spaulding and G. Simpson (New York, The Free Press, 1966).

Easthope, G., *A History of Social Research Methods* (London, Longman, 1974).

Engels, F., *The Condition of the Working Class in England* (St Albans, Panther Books, 1969; first published, 1845, first published in England, 1892).

Giddens, A., *New Rules of Sociological Method* (London, Hutchinson, 1976).

*Harper, W.M., *Statistics* (3rd edn, Plymouth, Macdonald and Evans, 1977).

Heath, A., *Social Mobility* (Glasgow, Fontana, 1981).

Hindess, B., *The Use of Official Statistics in Sociology* (London, Macmillan, 1973).

Huff, D., *How to Lie with Statistics* (Harmondsworth, Penguin Books, 1973).

Irvine, J., Miles, I. and Evans, J., *Demystifying Social Statistics* (London, Pluto Press, 1979).

Kent, R.A., *A History of British Empirical Sociology* (Aldershot, Gower, 1981).

Kuhn, T., *The Structure of Scientific Revolutions* (Chicago, University of Chicago Press, 1970).

Longford, E., *Eminent Victorian Women* (London, Weidenfeld and Nicolson, 1981).

Marx, K., *Capital*, Vol. I (Harmondsworth, Penguin Books, 1976; first published, 1867).

Mayhew, H., *London Labour and the London Poor* (London, Griffin, 1851).

*Mayntz, R., Holm, K. and Hoebner, P., *Introduction to Empirical Sociology* (Harmondsworth, Penguin Books, 1976).

Nie, N.H., Hadlai Hull, C., Jenkins, J.G., Steinbrenner, K. and Bent, D.H., *Statistical Package for the Social Sciences* (2nd edn, New York, McGraw Hill, 1975).

*O'Muircheartaigh, C. and Francis, D.P., *Statistics. A Dictionary of Terms and Ideas* (London, Arrow Books, 1981).

*Ott, L., Larson, R.F. and Mendenhall, W., *Statistics: A Tool for the Social Sciences* (3rd edn, Boston Mass., Duxbury Press, 1983).

Pahl, R., 'Playing the rationality game: the sociologist as a hired expert', in C. Bell and H. Newby (eds), *Doing Sociological Research* (London, Allen and Unwin, 1977).

*Reichmann, W.J. *Use and Abuse of Statistics* (Harmondsworth, Pelican Books, 1964).

Rowntree, S., *Poverty: A Study of Town Life* (London, Macmillan 1902).

Thompson, E.P. and Yeo, E., *The Unknown Mayhew* (London, Merlin Press, 1971).

Index